Alima Press

Las Vegas

The Emerald Rebels:

The Rise, Fall and Redemption of Philip Lynott and Thin Lizzy

Xaviant Haze

Table of Contents

Introduction

Saga of the aging Orphan

Shades of a blue Orphanage

Electric Vagabonds

Double axe Attack

Fighting!

G. I. Joe is back in Town

The Rockers

A bad Reputation

Living Dangerously

Black rose of Death

Solo in Chinatown

It's getting Dangerous

Ride the Lightning

The Sun goes Down

Redemption

Notes

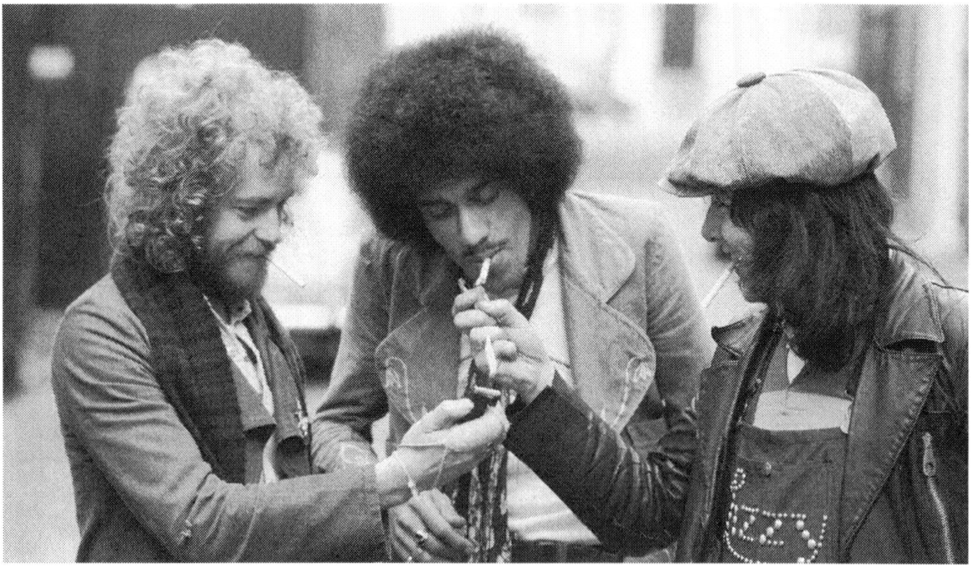
IZZY

Introduction

Most bands come and go through a revolving musical door, barely stepping out long enough to make a lasting impression. Some might even have a hit before fading back into obscurity. Record and thrift stores are full of albums to be listened to and pondered over by curious teenagers of future generations; bands lost in time wishing for immortality. Thin Lizzy were immortals. Nearly thirty years after their implosion you can turn on your television and still hear "The Boys Are Back in Town" rumbling out of some commercial advertisement, or rocking some hundred million dollar stadium during a football game. Their remarkable influence is everywhere, especially when you consider the impact they had on fellow musicians. From U2 to Metallica to Nirvana to the Darkness over three generations of rockers have made it clear that they owe a little something to Phil Lynott and his rebel group of musicians.

The Thin Lizzy story is a classic tale of excessive rock n' roll behavior. Overindulgence in girls, alcohol, and drugs provided the backdrop of a surreal tale that began in small Irish clubs in the 1960s and rose to packed stadiums by the late '70s. Thin Lizzy didn't just talk the talk; they walked the walk and rocked it even harder. Fronted by the classic line-up of bass-playing frontman Philip Lynott, drummer Brian Downey and guitarists Scott Gorham and Brian Robertson, Thin Lizzy soared to astonishing heights from 1975 to 1978 hitting their stride by releasing four classic albums in a row. These gems include their breakthrough LP Jailbreak, the beautiful concept album Johnny the Fox, the sonic equivalent of W.B. Yeats meeting Mozart at an Irish pub Bad Reputation and the speaker busting Live and Dangerous (recently voted by the BBC as the greatest live album of all time) all brawling their way into the UK Top 20.

In 1979, they reached their peak with their most successful album Black Rose no doubt inspired by the return of the legendary Irish guitarist Gary Moore. But Moore quickly left the group, disgusted by the band's inability to clean up its drug habits. The bad habits remained. Phil Lynott branched out by doing a solo album Solo in Soho in 1980 and later on that year produced and wrote another Lizzy classic, Chinatown. However, the critics were unkind, and the song and video "Killer on the Loose" coincided with an actual spate of serial murders in England, which nixed any chance of Lizzy reclaiming its commercial glory. The inability to hit the charts again and the recognition that they had not made it America began to wear down the band's members, who all felt they were going nowhere. Thin Lizzy wasn't getting any bigger.

By 1983, they had become victims of their self-destruction. Financially strapped and trapped by drug abuse the mighty Lizzy train was coming to a halt. After releasing their 13th and final studio album Thunder and Lightning (a metal album when everyone else was doing punk) they decided to retire the band in a farewell tour. On September 4, 1983 tears fell as Thin Lizzy played their final set at the Zeppelin field in Nuremberg, Germany. It' believed that Lynott never wanted to end Lizzy and that he just needed a break.

Whether Phil believed this or not is up for debate; what isn't debatable is that after Thin Lizzy split up, he never recovered from it. Throwing salt on the wound, add the breakup of Lizzy with a divorce and separation from his wife and kids. Lynott had now lost both of his families, and his heroin addiction consumed him. Phil's last chart appearance came in 1985 when old friend Gary Moore rescued him for the collaborative "Out in the Fields" single which shot as high as #5 in the UK. Jamming with his old friend from Ireland was the last time the majority of the public would ever see Phil Lynott. The end came for Phil on January 4, 1986, after the Lizzy leader died from rock n' roll excess, resulting in blood poisoning and non-responsive organs. The 36-year-old left behind two daughters, a secret love child, a broken band, a mother who adored him, and a legion of fans shocked, saddened and heartbroken.

But as the years passed a magical thing happened, instead of fading into obscurity, Lizzy's legend grew. New generations of fans lured in by the cool album covers, beautiful harmonic guitar soliloquies, and intricate, deep, soulful poetry became new Lizzy fans. This trend continues today and rightfully so. In 2010, Universal records began remastering Lizzy's classic albums with Brian Downey and Scott Gorham overlooking the process. One of rock's biggest mysteries is why Thin Lizzy never crossed over to the big time in America? Maybe in the 21st century and twenty-five years after the death of their legendary front man, they might finally get a chance. America fascinated Phil; he wrote songs about American themes better than many American songwriters. But Ireland held a big part of his soul, and Phil was uniquely Irish. Ireland has the most poets per square inch than anywhere in the world, and Phil Lynott joins Yeats, Wilde and Byron as one of its greats. Every bit as Irish and every bit as talented Lynott evolved into one of the greatest poets of his generation. But fame comes at a price and for the little black boy on the Grafton street corner there would be many years of hardships and poverty before finally cashing in with a little Irish luck.

Saga of the aging Orphan

That crazed girl improvising her music

Her poetry, dancing upon the shore

Her soul in division from itself Climbing, falling she knew not where

Hiding amid the cargo of a steamship, her knee-cap broken, that girl I declare

A beautiful lofty thing or a thing heroically lost, heroically found

No matter what disaster occurred she stood in desperate music wound, wound,

And she made in her triumph where the bales and the baskets lay

No common intelligible sound But sang, 'O sea-starved, hungry sea

W.B. Yeats

World War Two was in full bloom when Ireland decided to claim neutrality and not get involved. However if you were a young American soldier in the 1940's there was a good chance that you might find yourself roaming the emerald isle with a military issued copy of A Pocket Guide to Northern Ireland tucked away in your camouflaged overalls. Over the first few pages, we learn that Ireland is a splintered land and that Hitler could be lurking just around the corner. It was probably your typical misty Irish morning when a young G.I. read:

YOU are going away from home on an important mission – to meet Hitler and beat him on his own ground. For the time being you will be the guest of Northern Ireland. The purpose of this guide is to get you acquainted with the Irish, their country and their ways. You will start out with good prospects. The Irish like Americans. Virtually every Irishman has' friends or relatives in the United States; he is predisposed in your favor and anxious to hear what you have to say. This, however, puts you under a definite obligation: you will be expected to live up to the Irishman's high opinion of Americans. That's a real responsibility. The people of Northern Ireland are not only friends, but also Allies. They are fighting by the side of England, the United States, and the rest of the United Nations. Thousands of Irishmen are hefting steel in the hot spots of the war, doing their share and more. It is common decency to treat your friends well; it is a military necessity to treat your allies well. Every American thinks he knows something about Ireland. But which Ireland? There are two Irelands. The shamrock, St. Patrick's Day, the wearing of the green — these belong to Southern Ireland, now called Eire (Air-a). Eire is neutral in the war. Northern Ireland treasures its governmental union with England above all things.[1]

It becomes immediately apparent that the Ireland most are familiar with lies in the leprechaun south, while the northern tip of the land of Eire remains an occupied territory with flags flown by a little stake in the ground courtesy of the English crown. As the G.I. finished the manual, he must think it ironic that Ireland was worried about German invaders when English invaders had already claimed a good stretch of Irish land. After the Second World War ended Ireland's economic outlook was dim, and the questionable pre and post war policies left the island nation in utter ruin. 1950s Irish society was very close-knit with over 90 per cent of the population being Catholic. A very high proportion of the young population immigrated to England to find work after the war. Southern Ireland, being punished for refusing to enter the war was left in economic ruin. These new immigrants joined the previous wave of Irish wanderers. Some 200,000 men from Southern Ireland volunteered during WW2 just to be able to live in England, where they could find a job if they were lucky enough to survive the war. With Ireland missing out on the post-war boom and tired of poverty and religious dogmas, scores of Irish youth began making the trip across the cold seas to England and seventeen year old Philomena Lynott was one of them.

Born in a section of Dublin known as the Liberties in 1930, Philomena Lynott was ten years old when the first bombings of neutral Ireland began. As panic spread, it would be an anxious four months before the Luftwaffe dropped bombs on the city of Dublin shortly after New Year's Day in 1941. Philomena and her family would ultimately survive the raids as German bombs destroyed churches, synagogues, and family homes. Four months later more German bombs were unleashed on Dublin, destroying homes in Ballybough, Summerhill Park, the Dog Pond pumping works, and damaging the President's home at Phoenix Park. The worst calamities were at North Strand between Seville Place and Newcomen Bridge where a German bombing spree wrecked the community, claiming the lives of 28 people, injuring over 100, and leaving over 400 people homeless. After the smoke had cleared from the war, jobs were few and far between for Philomena and her two elder sisters and elder brother. They decided to join RAF in England (a junior military service) and study nursing.

Philomena joined her sisters in Leeds but was called back to Dublin to help her mother who was having a baby late in life at 51 years of age. After Philomena's mother gave birth to a son named Peter, she was allowed to return to England. This time, working in the dreary town of Birmingham, she met an older man all too eager to woo the young virgin from Dublin. Cecil Parris was from Georgetown, British Guiana on the northern coast of South America. In 1947, he decided to move to New York, but fate intervened, and he never reached his destination. Unknown to him, the ship he hopped was bound for Britain and disembarked at Liverpool. A year later he met Philomena at a dancehall in Birmingham.

From a 2010 article in the Daily Mail, Philomena explains, "I never fell in love with him. It was a "happening". You've got to remember that I was 17 or 18, and I didn't smoke or drink, but we used to go to these dances. Philip's father came all across the dance floor and he asked for a dance and I couldn't refuse him." As the only man of color in the building it must have taken a lot of swag for the older Cecil Parris to approach the glowing Irish princess. About the possibility of shooting him down Philomena recalls, "I'll tell you why: it wasn't in my heart. He had walked the whole length of the floor and everybody looked at him. Remember, they didn't want black to be mixing with white. It was fate – something said to me to get up and dance. And when I danced, the floor got full of people. He was a good dancer. When the dance was over, I walked back to where all the women stood and they all backed off – I was a nigger lover." [2]

As a shunned Philomena made her way outside her friends began to hound her for dancing with a black man. Cecil protected her from any more harassment and afterward their brief courtship began. After taking her virginity Cecil bailed for London, leaving Philomena alone and pregnant. Philomena accepted her situation and went to work in the foundry at the Austin Motor Company, hiding her pregnancy with an old-fashioned corset. Because she wasn't married, having a baby out of wedlock in those days could get you tagged as a tramp, the lowest place on the totem pole of life for a girl barely 18. Because of her embarrassment Philomena kept her pregnancy a secret to her family and on a rainy morning was rushed alone from work to the hospital, "I was taken from the foundry in an ambulance to the hospital and I was 36 hours in labor…I just lay there, and I suffered in silence. Because nobody knew. None of my family knew that I was having a baby. I couldn't tell them, the shame was unmerciful."

Weighing nearly ten pounds, Philip Parris Lynott came into the world on August 20, 1949. Because she was poor and unmarried Philomena had been forced to move into the Selly Oak Home, once there, nuns tried to persuade her to give Philip up for adoption, feeding her a steady diet of guilt for having a black illegitimate baby. Philomena remembers the cruelty she suffered saying, "It was awful what they did to me in that place. They put me out to work in the shed because I was the lowest of the lowest – because I had a black baby. Even today, I live with a bad back because it was freezing working in the shed – it was a stone floor."

Eventually, she met a friend in a similar situation who persuaded her to go to Liverpool. Her living conditions barely improved and soon Philomena had another child out of wedlock. Cecil was long gone and Philomena was being buried under the extreme poverty she found herself in. She explains, "That was heavy. Because when I had the little girl, I was in digs, in slums, which was horrible. There was a welfare nun who used to visit and she said to me, "You're going home to Ireland at Christmas. Would you like me to look after Jeannette for you?" When I came back, she brought Jeannette back to me and she was dressed up and she was full of toys. She said, "Guess where I took her? I took her to a schoolteacher and his wife". They were trying to adopt a little girl. Philomena, why don't you let your little girl have a break? Because you're going to have to spend the rest of your life living in the slums. This child will have a wonderful life." It wouldn't be long before Philomena would have to give up Philip as well.

Her bundle of brown joy, now four years old, was sent to live with his grandmother, Sarah Lynott, in the south Dublin suburb of Crumlin while his mother stayed in Manchester. At first his grandmother had to make excuses to the neighbors for him, claiming he was the son of one her daughter's friends and that his mother had died. Eventually, this lie wore off, and everyone had to accept the facts. Phil grew up with an adoring grandmother and a growing sense that he was unique. The young Phil Lynott's first memories were of Dublin, and eventually all of Phil's influences and future poetic musings would serve as a direct result from growing up in Crumlin with his grandmother Sara. The impact she had on him would be evident later in his life when he named his first-born daughter after her.

Despite being another black child without a father, growing up in Dublin with a positive family influence served him well. Philomena's brothers and sisters were all very good to Phil and he never suffered from lack of love, even his uncle Peter who was just a few years older than him, had a big impact on Phil's life. Peter was the first one in the family to play the guitar and spend his money on records. Soon Phil got a guitar and began to roam around Dublin seeking out musicians and poets. He didn't have to go far as it turned out that one of his friends from school happened to be a pretty good drummer. Phil had known Brian Downey for years before the idea of them ever jamming together materialized. Now the two fourteen-year-olds suddenly had a purpose in life. From that moment on they would were locked at the hip, with Brian's drumming accompanied by Phil's Elvis inspired crooning.

It was the early sixties and their first band together was named the Black Eagles. They played the chart songs of the day and became locally popular in part because of Phil's exotic appeal. He stuck out like a sore thumb in white Dublin. But the racial prejudice he faced while he was younger had worn off. Now he was the cool black Irish kid. The Black Eagles eventually became popular enough to travel the country, opening up for some of the biggest showroom bands in Ireland. Lynott wowed audiences with his crooning abilities and was decades ahead of Michael Jackson when it came to controlling a crowd by wearing a glove on one hand. But the Black Eagles had broken up by the time Phil turned eighteen. Parting ways with Brian, Phil fronted the experimental jam band Kama Sutra for a few months before being asked by bassist Brush Shiels to join his band Skid Row. Shiels wasn't looking for a singer; he was more interested in a showman, admitting, "I didn't particularly want someone who could sing well. I just wanted someone who looked good. Philip was about the best-looking boy around, and I knew that with him fronting the band we'd get lots of attention from the girls."

In 1969, Skid Row released their first single "New Faces, Old Places" on an independent record label, marking Lynott's first appearance on vinyl. In 2006, a stash of early Skid Row demos was discovered in a craggy basement in Dublin. These rare demos were showcasing different crooning styles and would be the first time we get to hear Phil growing into what he would eventually become. These recordings are also important for being the earliest recorded strumming from Ireland's greatest guitarist and bluesman Gary Moore. A frequent contributor to the Thin Lizzy story, Moore was only 16 when he ditched his home in Belfast to work the blossoming rock scene in Dublin. Moore was a self-taught virtuoso and like many others he was turned on to rock and roll first through hearing Elvis Presley, and then via The Beatles. But it wasn't until seeing Jimi Hendrix and John Mayall's Blues breakers perform in his hometown when he was opened up to the rich world of the blues.

For both the sixteen-year-old Moore and eighteen-year-old Lynott, Skid Row marked their first real rock band experience. Moore connected promptly with Phil, and the two became quick friends as the band built a decent buzz following Brush Shiel's lead. At Phil's home in Crumlin, the pair would spend hours together smoking marijuana and listening to his Uncle Peter's record collection. But for Phil the Skid Row party was short-lived, ending when he left for England to have his tonsils removed. When Phil returned Shiels informed him that he was moving the group into a three-piece Cream type power trio, and there would be no room for him. Phil was disappointed at hearing the news, but it turned out that Shiels wasn't a total dick about the process. He recognized Phil's talent and agreed to teach him how to play the bass. Perhaps the biggest disappointment for Phil was realizing he wasn't going to be jamming with Gary Moore anymore.

The nineteen-year-old Lynott wasn't deterred and showed up at Shiel's house almost every day learning the bass and writing new songs and poetry. With fresh inspiration, he joined Brian Downey's blues group Sugar Shack but the band quickly broke up leaving Downey and Lynott once again out of work. Making the best of a bad situation they finally took the plunge and decided to create their own band together. They founded Orphanage, the precursor to Thin Lizzy, with bassist Pat Quigly and guitarist Joe Stauton in early 1969. Finally, Phil had the freedom to perform his original material, and his bass playing became so good he eventually took over that position as well. Their cover of "Morning Dew" became a minor hit in Ireland, and both Phil and Brian had improved to the point where some of the early Orphanage compositions later evolved into Thin Lizzy songs. But Orphanage and its various members were too busy indulging in the popular hippie practices of the time like smoking weed and tripping on LSD to be considered as anything more than a half-assed dysfunctional band. They did manage to pull it together during a riot of a jam one night in a smoky Dublin pub and watching through the haze was a man that would soon plug in his guitar and help electrify Thin Lizzy into creation.

Shades of a blue Orphanage

TWILIGHT, a blossom grey in shadowy valleys dwells

Under the radiant dark the deep blue-tinted bells

In quietness reimage heaven within their blooms

Sapphire and gold and mystery

What strange perfumes

What bright companions nod and go along with it!

Out of the teeming dark what dusky creatures flit

That through the long leagues of the island night above

Come by me, wandering, whispering, beseeching love

As in the twilight children gather close and press

Nigh and more nigh with shadowy tenderness

Feeling they know not what, with noiseless footsteps glide

Seeking familiar lips or hearts to dream beside

O voices, I would go with you, with you, away

Facing once more the radiant gateways of the day

With you, with you, what memories arise, and nigh

Trampling the crowded figures of the dawn go by

George William Russell

Gary Moore wasn't the only guitar shredding virtuoso from Belfast looking to break into the emerging rock scene in Dublin. Eric Bell spent years jamming through a progression of bands while working odd jobs like jarring pickles and lighting streetlamps. By 1967, he had paid enough dues to gig briefly alongside the legendary Van Morrison in Them. After leaving Them, Eric eventually ended up doing showband tunes in The Dream and despite having a hit with "I Will see you there" decided to ditch the ballrooms for an attempt at forming a power trio. All he needed was a good drummer and a bassist. Bell spent months scouring the pubs in the Dublin rock circuit looking for possible candidates to join him on his rock n' roll fantasy. But it turned out that a chance encounter amplified by the magical powers of LSD would provide the answers he was looking for. Maybe it wasn't a chance encounter after all.

Sitting in the Bailey pub Bell and his friend the keyboardist Eric Wrixon looked over an advertisement announcing that Orphanage would be playing at Romano's in a few hours. At this point, Phil Lynott's Orphanage was more of an experimental jam band, and you never knew how many members would be in the group on any given night but regardless of this Brian Downey's drumming and Phil's folksy Celtic poetry was the musical buzz of Dublin. Sensing the potential good vibes of the night Eric Wrixon pulled out a couple tabs of acid. Having never done acid before, Eric Bell reluctantly placed the acid onto his tongue. It dissolved while Wrixon assured him that the night would be a blast, the two lads from Belfast stepped onto the wet Dublin streets slowly strutting towards destiny.

Once inside the club the effects of the acid began to hammer Bell's senses, plugging him in as he watched Orphanage take the stage. Phil's singing, swagger and instantly recognizable stage presence hit Bell like a ton of bricks. He thought to himself or mumbled out loud "Who is that?" he didn't need acid to know that Philip Lynott was by far the coolest dude he had ever seen. But when the sonic pounding of Brian Downey's drums kicked in he knew something magical was happening. After the set ended Bell wandered backstage and knocked on Orphanage's dressing room door. He was invited in by Phil and Brian and just walked around the room laughing, trying to explain that this was his first trip. Eventually, the laughter stopped, and he asked Phil and Brian if they wanted to start a group together with him and keyboardist Eric Wrixon. Phil was excited about this sudden newfound opportunity and had already heard good things about Bell's playing from Gary Moore. Feeling that Orphanage had gone on as far as it could, he convinced Brian that forming another band would give them some new creative energy and inspiration. When Phil busted out some funky bass riffs, Eric Bell realized that he had gotten what he wanted, and after this LSD fueled encounter none of them would ever be the same.

The lads met at Eric's flat where they listened to demos, got stoned and felt each other out. Word quickly spread around Dublin that an Eric Bell and Phil Lynott super group was forming. The news became official after Eric named the band after a Dandy's comic strip character named Tin Lizzie. With a little joking by Phil, the name became Thin Lizzy, knowing that the Irish couldn't pronounce the 'H' gave the band their first mischievous doing. With the band named and a new identity all they needed was a place to jam. Phil thought it was a great idea for the band to live together. If they were going to be an electric outfit then, they would need to be together as much as possible, jamming, drinking, smoking and chasing chicks. What more would you want to do as hard rocking dudes barely twenty years old? The band living in a communal setting together is a rock n' roll practice emulated for decades. When Guns n' Roses first started they all lived and jammed in a tiny storage space in Los Angeles.

From the Guns n' Roses History blog:

Desperately poor, the fledgling band struggled to survive in the streets of LA. Axl and Slash eventually rented a single 15 x 20 foot storage unit off Sunset & Gardner that shared a community bathroom. They called it the Sunset & Gardner Hotel and Villa. Axl took the back room that had a lockable door; he kept his space immaculate. Izzy and Steven stole lumber from a construction yard where Robert John worked some 2x4s and they built a queen size loft above the drum kit for Slash to sleep on…On a typical night, Axl or Slash would be getting laid in the loft while the other would be passed out between the drum kit and an amp, while assorted friends drank and used drugs in the alley until sunrise. It quickly became a den for sex, drugs and rock n' roll. [3]

Take a good look at Axl Rose's shirt during his iconic performance at the Ritz in 1988. Yep, it's a Thin Lizzy tee. Axl even had the cover from the album Black Rose (an album we'll discuss in a later chapter) tattooed on his shoulder. Rose told a reporter after a show at CBGB'S in 1991 that Philip Lynott was like his father growing up and Axl's biggest disappointment in life was not getting a chance to meet Phil and show him his rad tattoo before he died. But for Phil and his newly formed outfit, it would be many decades before they had a chance to influence America's greatest rock band.

Phil Lynott was a stylish dude and instant charmer who could lure anyone to his cause with overflowing charisma. The boys found that out quickly when they met him at a cafe dressed up in a fancy suit and tie. Phil flashed his devilish smile and jangled keys in the air. He had gotten them a place to jam and live together. Phil had somehow managed to rent the upstairs half of an apartment building in an upscale north Dublin neighborhood of Clontarf. On Castle Avenue and 'ascal an ohaissleain' Thin Lizzy got its start. However, the jam pad became a crash pad, and the constant flow of traffic and noise had irritated the neighbors to the point of them passing around a petition to have the boys evicted. They made their first official live performance at St. Anthony's Hall in early January 1970. Four months later, a small label Parlophone expressed an interest in signing the four-piece. The optimistic crew made their way to Baggott Street and entered Trend's Studio. In exchange for free studio time the band recorded studio owner's John D'Ardis song, "I need you" which wound up on the B-side to Lynott's A-side composition "The Farmer". Released on July 31st 1970, Thin Lizzy's very first single sank into oblivion, and legend claims that half of the 500 misspelled copies pressed were melted down and recycled. It's interesting to note that Phil's lyrics for "The Farmer" weren't even about Ireland or its myths, but a song about the American Wild West. The record flopped and to their surprise Parlophone dropped them. By this time, they had kicked out keyboardist Eric Wrixon and were evolving into a full-blown power trio.

Gigging wherever and whenever they could, the band was able to land a manager named Brian Tuite. Tuite arranged a gig for them backing up a popular Irish crooner that Frank Rodgers from Decca Records in London was coming over to see. The plan worked as Rodgers, impressed by Lizzy's playing, decided to sign the boys if they agreed to relocate to London. Thin Lizzy eagerly crossed the Irish Sea and once in London went to Decca's studios to record their debut album. Things were finally looking up for Phil and his band. In swinging London Phil had a ball spending money on clothes he found in second-hand stores. An instant fashionista, he fit right into the London scene. For Phil, London presented more than a chance to record his debut album, it was also a chance to walk in the footsteps of his hero Jimi Hendrix. For many white kids in the UK and Ireland Jimi Hendrix was the first young black man they saw on English television. His appearances were electrifying and sent shockwaves throughout England proper.

Suddenly guitarists like Eric Clapton and Jeff Beck who were deemed the new electric gods became obsolete overnight. Here were all these white boys in England practicing off of old chess records from Chicago blues acts and thinking they were good until a real life bluesman from America appeared out of nowhere and blew everyone out of the water. For Phil it was a sign from above, a cosmic confirmation that a black man could rock and be accepted and respected by everyone. Jimi Hendrix provided the source of inspiration Phil needed, and his natural born talent provided the rest. Now here he was 21 years of age and following in his hero's path by recording his first album in the drizzly city of London.

Recorded over a stretch of six days the bands self-titled debut Thin Lizzy was released to little fanfare in the spring of 1971, despite being given a break by popular Radio One DJ John Peel. Lizzy gained a decent amount of airplay and buzz began to build based on their crunching live sets seen throughout clubs in London like Baise's, and Ronnie Scott's. Thin Lizzy toured up and down England, but the album flopped. Mostly a mix of Phil's Celtic poetry and uneven jam sessions the album is an interesting listen to the group's first recording attempt. Eric Bell was no doubt the leader of the band at this point. He was older, more confident and performing at a higher level than his band mates. He even wrote one of the album's best songs, "Ray Gun" a spacey blues jam that Phil sings beautifully on. Eric's riffs and Brian's drumming do stand out, but Phil's singing is still a little shy and enclosed within. However, his songwriting was beginning to take form. In the song "Honesty is no excuse" Phil laments about a lost love.

Up till now I used to pass my time drinking beer so slowly

Sometimes wine no God, air, water or sunshine

And honesty was my only excuse I took your love and I used it

Up till now my youthful stage a useless rage, a torn out page, a worn out gauge

A dirty shade, a big charade, a has been made and honesty was my only excuse

I took your love and I used it I never, I never, I never up till now my love life

Few sweet kisses, a little missus, a fork and knife

A happy home, a hand to hold, a land to roam and honesty was my only excuse

The album contains many songwriting contenders including "Eire" (about an ancient Viking invasion in Ireland) "Remembering" (lost love) "Look what the wind blew in" (about spending a lifetime working in the factory) "Dublin" (Phil was homesick) "Saga of the ageing orphan" (about growing up without a father) but perhaps the best song and the most hopeful of all the songs they recorded was "Things ain't working out down on the farm". With this song, they nailed the harmonies that would become their signature trademark in years to come. All the parts came together on this song about a guy down on his luck…

There goes Moses carrying his bible book

Never has a problem, just has a cup its good clean alcohol and it fills you up

And here I go laughing like a fool, yeah things ain't working out down at the farm

Got no bag or baggage or love to keep me warm

And I ain't been in trouble since the day I was born

Things ain't working out down at the farm

Despite the album's commercial disappointment, Decca kept them under contract. Unsure about financing a second album, Decca released an EP entitled New Day on Philip's 22nd birthday in August 1971. The EP was a reworking of four of their best songs and it warmed over Decca enough to green-light production of Thin Lizzy's second album at Lane Lea Studios in Wembley. Shades of a Blue Orphanage was released in March of 1972. Phil, Eric, and Brian were all disappointed with the results. Feeling they weren't given enough time to come up with better compositions or mix the album. Despite their lack of faith, there are some great tracks on the album. The seven-minute Bedouin inspired jam "The rise and dear demise of the funky nomadic tribes" single handily makes up for the jaggedness of the entire album. It's a blistering example of great free form jazz scattered drumming and sharp bluesy guitar stabs. Phil's lyrics aren't bad either…

Out of sight, do it, the people rose and set off for the sun

At night they read their star signs a people proud for they know their kingdom come their skin was tanned by moonshine

I know now why they gone and it's all past, there comes a European his love was good but his lust, it lingered last and stuck like a devil demon

On lonely nights you can hear the distant call and good hearts hear the rhythm

And now I know pride before a fall on the road to freedom

The album also contains a forgettable tune inspired by Elvis "I don't want to forget how to jive" and a lovely song dedicated to Phil's grandmother "Sarah". The best musical moment besides the Nomadic track is the cut "Babyface" although Phil's lyrics don't add much, his scream and aggression make it listenable, but Brian's drumming accompanied by Bell's shredding is top notch, and one of the highlights of the album. The track "Call the police" might be the first real Thin Lizzy track ever recorded. It captures the vibe perfectly for what the band would become. The album closes with "Shades of a blue orphanage" a beautiful poetic ballad written by Phil…

When we were kids he used to go over the back wall into old Dan's scrapyard

Into the snooker hall where most us kids were barred an' into the Roxy and the Stella where film stars starred that's where me and Hopalong an' Roy Rogers got drunk and jarred and we might have been the savior of the men

The captured captain in the devil's demon den

And we might have been the magic politician in some kind of tricky position

Like an old, old, old master musician we kept on wishin'

"Buffalo Gal" is the stand out track of the album, mostly due in part to Phil's excellent story-driven lyrics and a peculiar chorus arrangement. Oddly enough, it was another song inspired by scenes from classic American imagery. This time about a young Southern belle on the range…

Buffalo Gal you've had your fun

Your button's undone and the time's right for slaughter

Buffalo Gal you're thirsty and there's no more water

Like the lamb on the altar

And it's sad to see you looking down and feeling blue

Try your best to get on up and see it through

In a while you might smile and see the sun

Oww, the day has begun and Buffalo Gal they're closing down the old dance hall

Ummm, Buffalo Gal, what we gonna do now?

Buffalo Gal due to these circumstances there's no more dances

Buffalo gal all your chances of further romances

Will have to be nil 'til I can get it sung

At a meeting at Decca's offices, the trio was told that a German businessman had offered Decca money for Thin Lizzy to record an album of Deep Purple hits. Decca agreed as Thin Lizzy's second album wasn't exactly setting the charts on fire, and they needed all the money they could get out of what appeared to be a bad investment. Phil and the gang were paid a thousand pounds to record the entire album in one day. Irish singer Benny White handled the vocals as Phil played the bass and sang back-up. Thin Lizzy's name was omitted from the credits and a picture of a totally different band even graced the album cover. Lizzy's Milli Vanilli-esque A Tribute to Deep Purple was released in January 1973 to little acclaim and soon the boys were back on the road touring Europe. Thin Lizzy's managers Ted Carroll and Chris Morrison were able to convince Chas Chandler to let Thin Lizzy open up in support of the highly popular acts Slade and Suzi Quatro. This tour was a defining moment for Thin Lizzy. Chas Chandler discovered Phil's hero Jimi Hendrix, and knew what it took to make a rock star. His current band Slade was the biggest act touring on the current rock circuit.

When Thin Lizzy hit the stage, they must have been a little shocked at the size of the crowd. They didn't pay it any mind and drove into their set as they normally did. But something was wrong; they weren't getting the right kind of response from the crowd. They suddenly realized that this was the big time, and they weren't ready for it. With chants of "We want Slade" drowning out their set, Lizzy and the boys played out their remaining tunes and sloshed backstage with their heads hanging. To make matters worse Phil got a scolding from Chas Chandler, who told him in unflattering words that if that's what their set was going to be like every night then they might as well just pack it up and head home. Phil was close to crying, his dreams nearly crushed by someone he admired. But he didn't let it get to him, now more determined than ever he began experimenting with poses and throwing 'shapes' while playing in front of the large crowds that Slade had provided them. Eric Bell and Brian Downey began to notice the gradual change of the normally reserved shy Phil over the course of the tour. Phil was slowly starting to become the rocker.

However, they were all broke, and as they sat in the Decca records office, they were reminded of the fact. Told in no uncertain terms that if they didn't come up with a hit single, their days at Decca were over. Thin Lizzy retreated back to their practice space situated in an old London pub. Depressed and homesick they began to mess around, searching and hoping for some musical inspiration. Facing their third strike, the boys from Dublin were in desperate need of a little Irish luck.

Electric Vagabonds

God knows I have it in my mind

The white house with the golden eaves

God knows since it is left behind

That something grieves and grieves

God keep the small house in his care

The garden bordered all in box

Where primulas and wallflowers are

And crocuses in flocks

God keep the little rooms that ope

One to another, swathed in green

Where honeysuckle lifts her cup

With jessamine between

God bless the quiet old grey head

That dreams beside the fire of me

And makes home there for me indeed

Over the Irish Sea

Katharine Tynan

By the end of 1972, Thin Lizzy had toured up and down England attracting a cult audience and gaining a rep as a crunching live act. Despite this stellar live rep their albums had flopped, they were poor as shit and had been told by their record company to come up with a hit or their days with them were over. Feeling immensely homesick and uninspired by ever-present metallic clouds and nonstop rain the boys tinkered with their instruments and tried to drum up inspiration inside the Duke of York pub. Phil and Eric passed a joint back and forth while Brian read a comic book in between tokes. After fogging up the place, Phil picked up a six-string Fender Telecaster and began to fool around with old Irish folk tales like "Seven drunken nights" and "Mary from Dun Low" before stumbling onto the classic Irish ballad "Whiskey in the jar" where Eric Bell joined in on the strumming for basically something to do. As the duo experimented a vibe inside the pub began to grow and by the time their road manager Ted entered the room to set up and rearrange some speakers it was clear to him that Lizzy was on to something. Phil didn't think so and reassured Ted that they were only messing around.

For Phil, the idea of rocking up an old Irish song sounded dreadful but Ted reminded the boys that their next single was due in only five weeks. Phil was confident that his original composition "Black boys on the corner" would make a great A-side and they quickly pounded out the tune to the delight of the producer Nick Tauber. After a short break to catch their breaths and fire up some hash Nick asked them about the song for the B-side of the single to which Phil responded, "I don't know." Their manager had been chirping in their ears that "Whiskey in the jar" sounded good, and Phil reluctantly agreed to record the song as the B-side to "Black boys on the corner". Brian played the drums and Phil ditched the bass for an acoustic six string, the same instrument that Eric was also playing. They recorded an acoustic take of "Whiskey" and at the end of the session Eric took a cassette of the song home to work out the electric guitar arrangements and melodies. Eric listened to it in a stupefied silence. It took two weeks for him to find the inspiration that he needed to make "Whiskey" a classic. He heard a song by the Chieftains that had epic an Irish pipes feel to it and he mimicked an electric guitar version of the pipes to provide the chilling intro. After nailing the beginning Eric started to think about the commercial and pop musical qualities that were needed to make a chart-topping hit and began repeating notes and coming up with a steady stream of constant chords that were very commercially sounding. By the time he banged out the solo he knew that he had figured out the riddle to making "Whiskey" a hit and phoned up Phil to tell him the good news.

Phil was relieved at hearing the sound of Eric's enthusiasm and welcomed the news happily. Everyone was riding Phil's back - the producers, their manager, and the record company all were pissed that Eric was two weeks behind schedule and wasting everyone's time. Phil was confident that Eric could pull it off and told everyone to chill out. He was correct. When Eric joined Phil, Brian and Nick at the recording studio and played the opening riffs of "Whiskey" everyone's hair on the back of their necks stood up. You can still get the same effect by listening to the song more than thirty years later. The single was cut, pressed, and shipped out but went nowhere. For five weeks, all they could say about their Irish folk-rock experiment to everyone that pushed for it was "I told you so." But the ingenious marketing savvy of their manager Chris Morrison began to turn the tide in Lizzy's favor when he sent out little bottles of whiskey with every copy of the 45 inch single to various DJ's. It worked, and the song began getting airplay all over the UK but to Lizzy "Whiskey" was already written off as a lost cause.

They were booked on a dreadful tour of Germany and played wine bars and other various locations they couldn't stand. The tour went so bad that both Phil and Eric were drunk and stoned out of their minds so much that they ended up getting into a fight with one another at their Hotel. The police were called, and the boys narrowly escaped being tossed into jail. They made up and apologized to each the next morning, but Brian Downey was sick of the whole affair and threatened to quit the band altogether. They felt like they were going nowhere and that Lizzy was doomed to be a failure. While waiting for their next gig, the boys got a telegram from London congratulating them. They thought it was a joke being played by their managers but suddenly grasped that it was very real. The telegram informed them that "Whiskey" had reached #25 on the English charts, and they needed to get their asses back to London pronto.

They couldn't believe it, canceled their remaining gigs in Germany and raced back to England with hopeful ambitions amidst curious feelings. By March of 1973 "Whiskey" had become a huge hit and eventually reached #6 on the UK charts while obviously landing at #1 in Ireland. It was also a top ten hit in Germany and gave Thin Lizzy their first dose of massive exposure. When they appeared on Top of the Pops for the first time, it was a huge deal, not only for the boys but also for the whole country of Ireland. Phil loved it and soaked it up. He had had finally made it and basked in the newfound fame and adulation. Phil, Brian, and Eric reaped the rewards and acquired more drinks, smoke and groupies then they had ever had before. And best of all Lizzy was booked into top-notch spots fit for their rocking ways.

With a bona fide hit on their hands, they gigged for three months straight before heading in the studio that summer to begin work on their third album. Recorded in London Vagabonds of the

Western World was the band's most confident, polished and solid work to date. It combined the psychedelic blues vibes of a Hendrix album mixed with Lizzy's blends of Celtic folk and experimental late 60's jam-band hippie soundscapes. Phil's lyrics continued to improve and by Vagabonds he had truly come into his own as a songwriter and mushrooming poet of serious potential. Eric Bell's guitar powers were at their full peaks, and Brian Downey's drumming was starting to morph into a signature style. Phil wanted to make sure that Vagabonds stood out and asked his old friend from Dublin the iconic artist Jim Fitzpatrick to help out with the album cover. Jim and Phil both had a love of comic books and decided that Vagabonds should have a cover similar to the style being currently used by Marvel. Jim designed an epic otherworldly sci-fi album cover that is still admired to this day. When the album hit the shelf it had no problem standing out and was indeed the coolest cover art done in 1973. It gave the original Lizzy fans an extra incentive to buy the album and no doubt inspired thousands of more fans who might have been on the fence until seeing the cover to Vagabonds of the Western World.

The album opener, "Mama Nature Said" a rolling slide guitar blues composition about destroying the Earth and other environmental issues way before it was a popular thing to talk about makes clear that to the listener that the spacey album cover wasn't just a gimmick. You were about to be taken on a rewarding musical journey. From Eric's superb slide driven solo to the echo-ized organ stabs from Jan Schelhass, a member of Gary Moore's band, "Mama Nature" is an excellent opening number. Phil's lyrics were ahead of time and presented a philosophy still sadly ignored by most of the world today. Written a full twenty years before bands like R.E.M began to raise conscious awareness about environment issues, Phil's ode to Mother Nature shows true poetic merit and substance…

Mama Nature said "its murder what you've done"

I sent you forth my brightest world

Now it's nearly gone

Birds and bees been telling me you can't see the forest for the trees

You cover up your lies with sympathies

And I got no solutions to your persecution

Mama Nature said "You're guilty of this crime"

Now it's not just a matter of fact But just a matter of time

Cruel will be the vengeance so savage is the deed that's done

And I've got no solutions to your own pollutions

The next track on the album is an ode to Frank Zappa called "The Hero and the Madman". Narrated by DJ David 'Kid' Jensen, the song is an unevenly mixed story that fuses spoken word bits alongside some solid musical parts (Brian's percussion work is great) that eventually leave the listener confused. It was a good effort to Zappa up the piece but ultimately the song falls flat, despite an excellent bass line by Phil, a blistering solo from Eric and some inventive mixing and overdubbing. "Hero" was a complex attempt at musical theater that almost worked and the first song that signaled the oncoming crackup of lead guitarist Eric Bell. During the initial recording Eric thought, "Holy fuck. This song is about me!" and it drove him into overindulging alcohol and hash to the point of a quick untimely burnout. Eric's private mental struggle aside, Phil's mythological tale of a cursed fatherless child who seeks a wizard to break his curse is another one of Phil's early songwriting gems...

If I recall you're the actor

Who followed the stars

Searching for the lost city of Mars

Hoping time would heal the scars

Knowing fate held no bars

Are you the one that I think you are?

Are you the hero or are you the madman?

"Slow blues" begins as a straightforward Chess Records romp with bombastic drums, piercing guitar jolts and the wailing vocals of a troubled soul from down deep in the delta. But when the groove gets going Phil's thumping bass riff makes the track more of a funk number than a traditional blues song, despite the obvious blues infested shredding by Eric Bell. The album's next track is the most important song on Vagabonds and would help lay the groundwork for what the 70's would have in store for the Thin Lizzy brand. An instantly recognizable and classic Lizzy tune, "The Rocker" was an obvious choice for the albums lead single. An eventual machismo fan favorite that remained in the band's live set up until the end "The Rocker" is bar none a great song about rock n' roll and a precursor to "The Boys are back in town" and "Warriors".

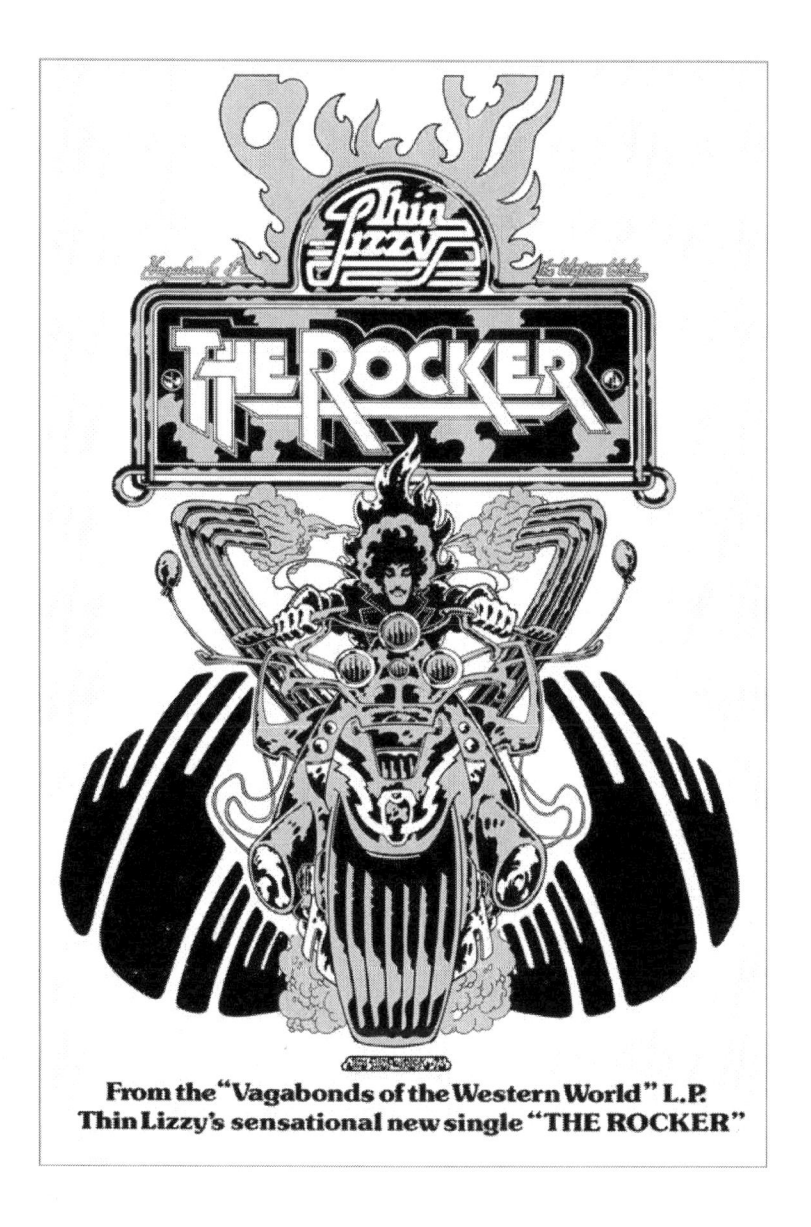

Although relatively simple, Eric Bell's blistering guitar solo (perhaps his best) and Phil's catchy hook, confident delivery, storytelling capability and brilliantly arrogant vocals provide the track with an everlasting appeal. Written by Phil and inspired by real "Rockers" that he would see buying records and out cruising London on their motorcycles, it was released around Christmas of 1973. Unfortunately "The Rocker" was lost in the Yuletide rush and to the shock of everyone failed to chart higher than #38. It was a hugely unexpected blow to the band and especially Phil who was hungry for fame and desperately wanted to get back on Top of the Pops. It almost seems unbelievable now that "The Rocker" failed to make an impact on the charts when released. Real life characters and the fact that his manager Ted worked at the 'Rock on Stall' record store inspired Phil's spot on lyrics…

I am your main man if you're looking for trouble

I'll take no lip 'cause no one's tougher than me

If I kicked your face you'd soon be seeing double

Hey little girl, keep your hands off me 'cause I'm a rocker

Down at the juke joint me and the boys were stompin'

Bippin' an a boppin', telling a dirty joke or two

In walked this chick and I knew she was up to something

I kissed her right there out of the blue

I said - Hey baby, meet me I'm a tough guy

Got my cycle outside, you wanna try?

She just looked at me and rolled them big eyes

And said, "Ooh I'd do anything for you 'cause you're a rocker"

That's right I'm a rocker

The album's title track "Vagabond of the Western World" is another spaced out blues folk tale that succeeds where "Hero" failed. Equipped with an Irish inspired vocal scat 'tura-lura-lie' it is another homage to Phil's love of Irish mythology. From a 1977 review in Melody Maker:

The title track of 'Vagabond of the Western World' where Lynott admits that the tale of the Vagabond was a rip off from Tir Na Nog (Land of the Young) and every other mythological Irish story. The song was to describe the charm that Ireland possesses, where people will pay you a compliment even if you are their worst enemy. On the same song, Lynott sings the 'tura lura loo's' that are usually associated with Irish folk songs. [4]

In the same article, Phil explained that he was trying to sing more in an Irish accent and listened to a ton of traditional Irish records. Even the title of the song was essentially ripped off from an obscure Irish play influenced by the actor Errol Flynn called Playboy of the Western World. It is another fine example of Phil taking old Irish themes and adding a modern and unique Lizzy flair that expands and enlightens the poetry…

I could tell you the story of a vagabond

A playboy of the western world

One day by chance he came upon

A fair young maid, a country girl

He told her that he loved her

And he took all of her silver

He told her that he needed her too

He said "Hey baby, you got eyes of blue"

But he was a vagabond

Blue eyes, oh baby blue, oh blue eyes

The kind of eyes that say "I do" eyes

The aching ballad "Little Girl in Bloom" was inspired by Phil's mother and the struggles that she went through before and after her unwanted pregnancy. A touching lyrical gem by Phil that was emotionally moving, the song is unquestionably one of the finest examples that proved the power trio had serious musical chops. Eric's fuzzy feedback intro blends into electric guitar echo chimes that gel perfectly with Phil's simplistic thudding bass. Phil's harmonic vocals in the chorus are hauntingly beautiful, and Eric's solo is soft, warm and equally romantic if not understated in its delivery. Phil's tale of a pregnant teenage girl, who has to tell her father the unexpected news, predates Madonna's "Papa don't preach" by fifteen years. It's incredible that on the same album were Phil roguishly declared that he was a tough rocker who would kick your face in without any hesitations; he was also able to show off an unbelievable soft, caring and sensitive side too. On "I'm Gonna creep up on you" Phil's bass is aggressive and Brian's drums thump, showing a fine example of how tight he and Brian Downey could get in a drum and bass sound off. Not to be outdone Eric Bell goes all out in a rousing wah-wah pedal driven solo that carries the song to its ending. Not much in the way of lyrics on this track, the thumping groove acts as the songs main force aided by the drawl of a repeated hook sung by Phil. Closing the album is, "A Song for while I'm away" an impressive love song written by Phil while touring. It was the first love song that he wrote that didn't embarrass him, and his excellent singing and vocal phrasings make the track a smart choice to close the album. It was lavishly produced and included a dominant drenching of lush background strings that were arranged by the accomplished Fiachra Tench. Downey's plodding slow groove based around panning hi-hats and accompanied by Bell's ringing guitar riffs; compliment Phil's sad troubadour vocals…

These words I wrote, play and sing to you

Do not convey the love I brought and bring to you

For this is a song for while I'm away

To say all the things I'd love to say

You are my life, my everything, you're all I have

You are my hopes, my dreams, my world come true

You're all I have Please heed me now these words I have to say

Now I'm headed for the border

You see this song it ends right at the start

I swore when I was younger No one would win my heart

And far away hills look greener still

But soon they'll all slip away

It's then I'll be returning

And I'll be coming home to stay

Despite taking their time in the studio and recording a solid album Vagabonds failed to chart upon release and Lizzy was sent back on the road to perform their only hit "Whiskey in a jar" which was stupidly left off the album somehow, an absolutely bad choice by both the record company and Thin Lizzy that no doubt led to the disappointing first week sales. Confident that the album was a serious work of musical art but depressed in knowing that their third album in a row was a dud upon release, Eric bell's drinking consumed him.

Phil and Brian sucked it up the best they could and without any choice in the matter the trio was shipped to Spain, Germany, Finland and Holland to perform "Whiskey" which they usually mimed for foreign television audiences. By the time, the tour reached back home to Ireland the power trio was exhausted, broke and uninspired. Their singles failed to hit and their album, despite its amazing cover and sound sailed over most people's heads. Soon sinking off the public's buying radar for good. Eric Bell went out of his mind by the whole experience. He drank from the time that he awoke, through the gigs and before falling asleep. Unlike Phil, He didn't want to be famous and grew sick of the record label suits and overblown expectations. All

Eric wanted to do was play the guitar, but even that had grown stale to him. Prescribed Valium and mixing it with booze and hash every day like a walking zombie didn't help him either. He didn't bother to practice or even tune his guitar during the gigs and Phil warned him a few times to straighten out but it all came to a head on a windy New Year's Eve night in Eric's hometown of Belfast. Eric Bell had lost all interest in music and the resulting paranoia of drugs, lack of sleep and massive amounts of alcohol turned his mind into mush. He even started to believe that his guitar was evil and had put a hex on his soul. Eric had drunk so much alcohol prior to the New Year's Eve gig in Belfast that when he took the stage he didn't even know what was going on or where he was and worst of all "Who the fuck he was?"

By Lizzy's third number, both Brian and Phil looked at Eric in confused horror as he began playing the riffs of a different song. Eric was oblivious. He heard voices in his head telling him that he would die if he didn't throw his guitar up into the air and leave. So that's what he did! To everyone's astonishment Eric tossed his guitar in the air and then walked over to his amps and kicked them over and stomped them out. He then walked off the stage and crawled on top of a bunch of gym mats where he collapsed with his mind blown. The audience thought it was part of the act, and Phil joked that Eric only went to get a drink and would be right back. But that ominous night in Belfast marked the final Thin Lizzy appearance of Eric Bell.

Old friend Gary Moore joined Phil and Brian for a few months of gigging and you were indeed lucky if you happened to see that brief Moore, Lynott, Downey, Thin Lizzy power trio live. Gary Moore soon left to continue his solo career and when Phil and Brian returned to England, they were greeted with the harrowing news that Decca Records had officially dumped them. The news was devastating and the two old buddies from Crumlin once again found themselves back at square one.

Now without a guitarist Phil was determined that they had better hire two next time just in case one quit. While Vagabonds was a commercial failure and marked the end of Eric Bell's tenure with Lizzy, the albums importance cannot be overlooked or underestimated. For starters, Eric Bell left his soul on the album and his powerful flash finger blues chops and experimental electric shredding has stood the test of time. To be honest, without Bell's work on "Whiskey" and his 'leaving it all on the table' output on the Vagabonds album, Thin Lizzy might not had ever been able to break through the barriers that it was now running full steam to face head on. Bell's contribution to the Lizzy legend isn't exaggerated; it was necessary and deserves praise.

Twenty years after his breakdown, American rock super group Metallica honored Bell's guitar virtuosity by covering "Whiskey" and introducing it to a whole new generation of rockers. Their cover of the song even earned them a Grammy nomination! Metallica's lead guitarist Kirk Hammet proclaimed that his version paled in comparison with Eric Bell's and it's universally agreed upon by Phil and others that no one can get the notes and sounds of "Whiskey" just right other than Bell. One night Phil Lynott was told by a reporter, "It'd be nice to hear 'Whiskey in the Jar' tonight." Phil could only respond with a laugh saying, "It'd be nice to play it too. Only the chosen few are called to hear that number! No, the thing is Snowy had an idea, right, he only heard it when we were in Ireland, and then Scott doesn't like playing it because it's Eric Bell, you know. It's like, you know, I can sing it, Brian can play the beat but that guitar, it's just Eric Bell, you know what I mean?"

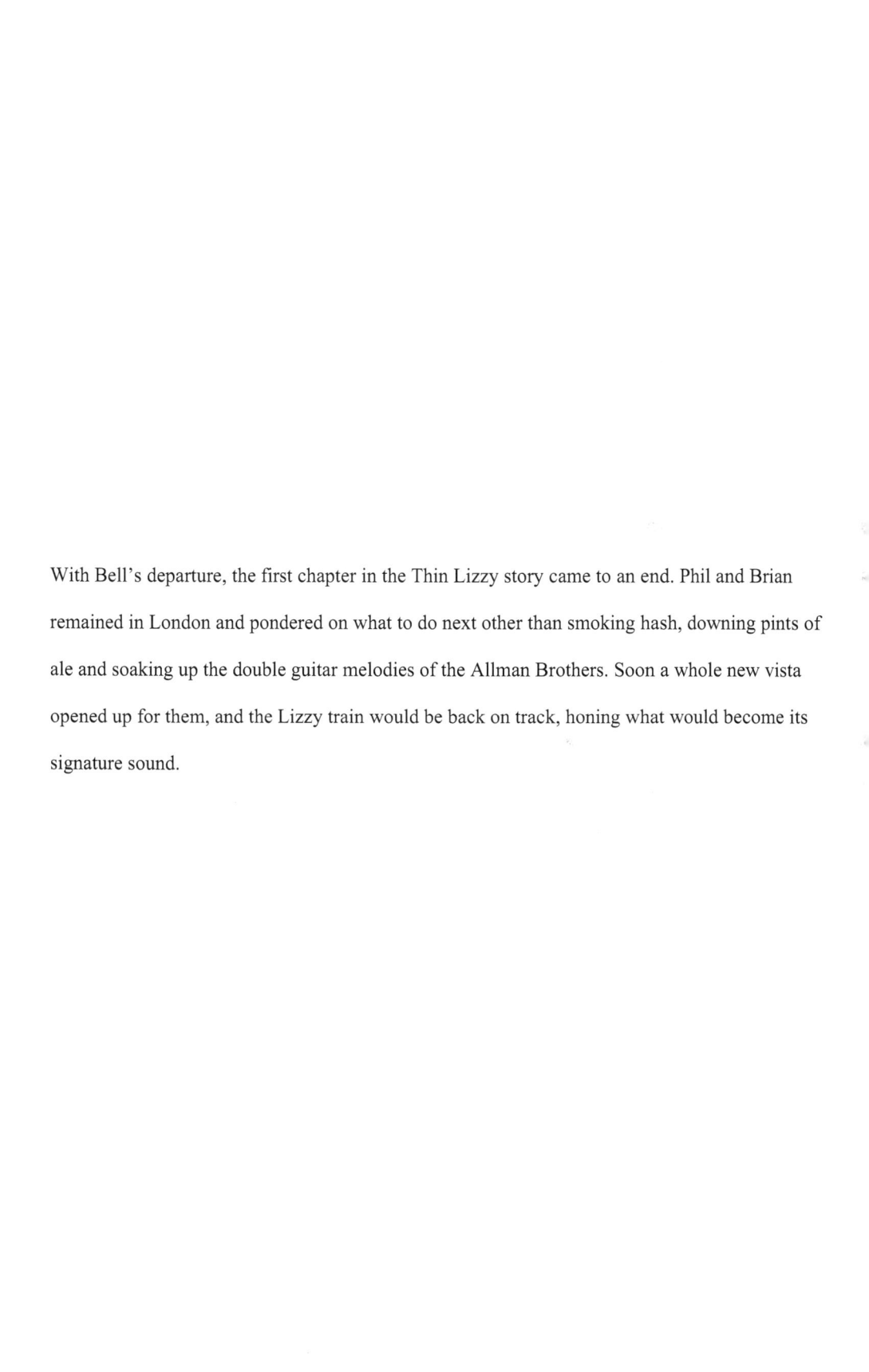

With Bell's departure, the first chapter in the Thin Lizzy story came to an end. Phil and Brian remained in London and pondered on what to do next other than smoking hash, downing pints of ale and soaking up the double guitar melodies of the Allman Brothers. Soon a whole new vista opened up for them, and the Lizzy train would be back on track, honing what would become its signature sound.

Double axe Attack

He heard there was a club of cheats

Who had contrived a thousand feats

Could change the stock, or cog a die

And thus deceive the sharpest eye

Nor wonder how his fortune sunk

His brothers fleece him when he's drunk

I own the moral not exact

Besides, the tale is false in fact

Wherein the moralist designed

A compliment on human kind

For here he owns, that now and then

Beasts may degenerate into men

Jonathan Swift

During the early months of 1974 Gary Moore jammed with Thin Lizzy for an Irish and English tour and fooled around with them in a couple of studio sessions. Although dropped by Decca Thin Lizzy still had one single left on their contract and was booked on a German tour to support it. The single "Little Darling" went nowhere and with no future prospects of any future record deals looming, all Lizzy could do was gig until the wheels came off. On February 9th, the power trio rocked the University of Glasgow. Watching this with wide eyes was a seventeen-year-old kid named Brian 'Robbo' Robertson. He had already heard all of the Lizzy singles and loved the Vagabonds album but now he had a chance to experience the sheer awesomeness of the live set. He was blown away! Later that night Robbo learned Thin Lizzy was staying at the Redhurst Hotel in Clarkston, so he dragged his guitar and his girlfriend to the Hotel with hopes of meeting anyone from the band. He succeeded in finding Brian, but Phil and Gary were out getting smashed somewhere together. Brian invited the kid and his chick into the Hotel room and they talked about music while smoking a joint. Robbo then started to play songs from the Thin Lizzy catalog for an astonished Brian. Robbo had been practicing Bell's Guitar methods since he was fifteen and was truly excited to be playing his guitar for the drummer of a band that he felt didn't get enough respect. Robbo left a happy kid and without any future expectations other than hoping Lizzy would soon come back to rock Scotland.

Lizzy were back on the road promoting "Little Darling" but Gary Moore left the group before they hit Germany, leaving them once again without a guitarist. Back in London Phil and Brian went to the Lyceum and watched Wishbone Ash destroy the place with their unique dueling double guitar sound style. After the show, they decided to reshape the band with two guitarists in the hopes of outdoing them. Andy Gee and John Cann were hired just before the tour started, and this short-lived incantation hit Germany to support another chart missing single. John already had achieved a little guitar notoriety with the success of Vincent Crane's Atomic Rooster and Andy jammed with the popular Steve Ellis band. The four lads that now formed the new Thin Lizzy caught a ferry from Harwich in the afternoon and arrived in Hamburg the next morning.

In Germany, guitarist Andy Gee's German background came in handy as he spoke the language fluently. His understanding of German at the Hotels, restaurants, pubs and social outings became more important to Phil than Andy's actual guitar playing. The tour dragged on, sometimes driving six hours a day, little crowds and an inexperienced German promoter began to make life on the road miserable for everybody involved. The two guitarists weren't on the same page and audio evidence of this disastrous tour can be heard on the bootlegs recorded in Frankfurt.

Brian was bored out of his mind knowing that this version of Thin Lizzy wasn't going anywhere and by the time the tour ended up in Holland John Cann left and Lizzy was back to a three piece. The power or the fury wasn't there, and a disillusioned Brian decided that he had enough. He halted the gigs, broke up the band and caught the next ferry from Belgium back to London where Phil had to beg him to continue seeing this Thin Lizzy thing through to the dire end. Brian never wanted to quit making music, and he and Phil were like brothers but he knew something had to be done in a hurry. He loved the idea of a twin guitar sound but what happened in Germany wasn't what he was looking for. Phil agreed and once again the two childhood friends from Dublin sat alone in their cold craggy flat, smoked hash, listened to records and thought of what to do.

By the summer of 1974, "Whiskey in the jar" and Lizzy's incessant touring had given Brian and Phil a tiny cult following and enough hope that fame and fortune were indeed accessible. But without a record deal and no money, the duo was no better off now then they were in 1968. Thin

Lizzy roadie and fellow Dubliner Frank Murray recalls the ill-fated German tour with Andy and John in Martin Popoff's book Fighting my way Back:

I don't think they quite got Lizzy. It was a strange thing; they were trying to replace Eric Bell, who is a very unique guitar player. And the songs they had at that time were also unique, in a certain way. And I think they came from a different background, musically; they wouldn't have had the subtleties of Eric, let's say. It wasn't working out the way it should've, or up to the standard we wanted it to be at. We were just trying to get through a tour. Again, we were doing a German tour that we'd been contracted to do. Also Philip wasn't the kind of guy who wanted to knock the road. He would just be like, 'Well, let's just audition some guitar players.' So we started auditioning, and ended up with John and Andy. But it was a very, very, weird tour as well. We went to all kinds of, I suppose, one-horse towns around Germany, the strangest towns, probably towns the Germans, people who live in Germany all their life, never got to. And maybe that wasn't helping things either. We were getting good crowds and things like that, but things just weren't working out down on the farm. (laughs) [5]

With their contractual obligations to Decca completed, Brian and Phil were on the verge of calling it a day but instead decided to spread the word in London that they would be auditioning for two guitarists. Inspired by Wishbone Ash, a group that by 1974 were already considered British rock pioneers; Thin Lizzy's new sound would also be going for the twin guitar effect. Soon a hundred hopeful guitarists lined up to audition for Phil and Brian. One of them was that teenage kid who played guitar for Brian Downey in a smoky Hotel room one night after a set in Scotland. A night Brian Downey could barely remember. When Robbo heard the news in a pub in Glasgow that Thin Lizzy was auditioning guitarists, he immediately sold everything he could and went to London in a rush with nothing but his guitar and the clothes on his back.

Brian 'Robbo' Robertson was born in Glasgow, Scotland in 1956 and raised to be a musical prodigy. By the time, he hit London Robbo had accumulated more than a decade of classical training on the cello and the piano. But what he wanted to do was rock, so despite the objections from his unsupportive and old-fashioned parents he adapted all of his classical musical training to be played on an electric guitar. With the help of a Scottish roadie that had seen the young guitar prodigy shred back home many times, Robbo was rushed into an instant audition upon arriving in London. It wasn't a big deal for him, and he had intuitively always known he would be playing guitar for Thin Lizzy.

Brian Downey sort of remembered the kid and Phil was amused that such a young bloke from Scotland had heard their records and was a huge fan. When the Scottish electric whiz kid plugged in his guitar and played, it was like a massive storm of Guitar angels shining a ray of light on Lizzy's future. Both Phil and Brian were blown away at what they heard and hired Robbo quicker than the snap of Phil's finger. With only one more guitarists needed, Phil and Brian were feeling a little bit better about the future as they prepared for the next wave of auditions, none of which could match the bar that had been raised by Robbo. Nobody was getting the job done, and the auditions dragged on to the point where Phil almost nixed the twin guitar sound style idea altogether, wanting to resort back to a power trio. But the final piece of the Lizzy puzzle came together a week later when a longhaired surfer looking dude from California walked in for a last minute audition.

Twenty-three-year-old Scott Gorham was from sunny Santa Monica, California and came over to England to audition for Super Tramp but didn't get the gig and had found little luck in joining other bands. Now on the verge of outstaying his visa he knew that Thin Lizzy presented the best chance for him to join a legitimate band and extend his work permit. The thought of returning to California a failure was horrific, he came to London to rock and infuse some of his laid back Californian Les Paul guitar style into the dated overly bluesy English scene. When he entered the staging area he saw that Robbo, Brian, and Phil were already on stage tuning up their instruments and looking miserable. Scott had run out of money and sold his Stratocaster, leaving him with only a cheap Japanese Les Paul knockoff. When Robbo and Brian saw it, they groaned. Phil was cool about it and told him to strap it on, Scott plugged in, let his fingers do the talking and the jam went off without a hitch.

Bringing a fresh dynamic to Lizzy with his laid back style, Scott got the job on the spot, mostly because of his awesome hair. He was hired to play rhythm guitar in support of Robbo until they could figure out how to harmonize new songs together. There was a vibe there during that initial rehearsal and Phil could feel it, this was going to be the Thin Lizzy line up the world would remember them by. Phil was no dummy, he knew that the look of the band was important, not only to the audience but also to the record company suits that were more concerned about image than actual talent. With the addition of Scott and Robbo, Thin Lizzy booked some gigs and worked out the kinks in a series of jagged live shows. Their first gig together was at the Lafayette in Wolver Hampton and they only played to about ten people. They were determined not to play any songs from the Bell era and were trying out new numbers by Phil alongside cuts from the Byrds and Bo Diddley with various results. On July 9th, they were finally getting used to each other and rocked the Marquee Club in London. Watching in the crowd and impressed by what they saw, executives from Phonogram signed Thin Lizzy to a new record deal on one of their smaller labels Vertigo records. Assigned to work with Bad Company producer Ron Nevison in studios in Worthing and London, the newly formed group began to get their feet wet and hone their future sound. Recorded during the summer of 1974, Lizzy's fourth album Nightlife was released on November 8th. They debuted the album and lead single "Philomena" during a big record release party organized by Vertigo at the Tara Towers Hotel in Dublin. It was a great night for the boys and all of Phil and Brian's friends and family came to the party. The next day they would be on the road promoting their new album and inspiring the blueprints for the workingman's band.

While on the road the boys put the album out of their minds and focused on the live shows and for good reason because Nightlife much like the band's previous three albums was also a flop and even worse had failed to chart. Their fourth album is unlike any album in their entire catalog, for many reasons of course and the fact that this was both Robbo and Scott's first ever record deal. They were still working out the kinks of the dueling guitar sound, while their coked out producer Nevison had no clue that Thin Lizzy were supposed to be hard ass rockers. Instead half the album comes out sounding like a mix of funk, soft rock and old school country music with only a hint of that Thin Lizzy hard rock magic. But to say that Nightlife isn't worth your time would be a joke, in fact this album shows that musically Lizzy were capable of pulling off any style. The album seems to be sort of a joke played on us by Thin Lizzy with a double meaning that seemed to sail over everyone's heads. On the album cover, again masterfully designed by Jim Fitzpatrick, Phil is shown as a panther that is about to stalk the streets of a far off metropolis. One gets the feeling that an epic sound clash of tough street anthems, all-night boozers and fights at the pub for fair maidens was going to be the feel of the album. This has been and pretty much is what we have come to expect from Thin Lizzy, so on an album that on the surface looks like a concept album of this idea, it is in fact the exact opposite! It's more of a night at home instead of a night on the town.

It's easy yet groovy, tame, but still rocks in parts and is underappreciated, but stands alone as Lizzy's most unique album. While the Bell era albums had an experimental psychedelic aspect to them, none of that can be found on Nightlife and despite it being sort of soft it works because it is just so fucking cool and laid back. But not to the point of putting you to sleep, Phil's bass work approaches P-funk levels and Brian's drumming snaps in neck bobbing pace to perfection. Phil's vocals and his chorus harmonies are starting to stand out, and there's no doubt that he has grown tremendously as a singer.

The mood of the album is what makes it so special; it's stylish and soulful and resonates on a completely different sonic level than Lizzy's first three albums. It goes places that they would never go again. While most of the album was constructed over the course of 1974, a point in which Phil was writing at a frenetic pace and his tremendous growth as a songwriter shows not only in the quasi-funk songs he did with Brian but also in the sentimental and heartfelt lyrics that litter the album. The leadoff track "She knows" is a laid back song dedicated to the Virgin Mary, it's a spiritual cut that's uplifting and sung beautifully. Scott Gorham's cool Californian style is all over the song and "She knows" even earned him his first co-writer credit.

The album's title track "Nightlife" was inspired by the Willie Nelson and B.B. King duet that Phil loved. The song is a lush musical piece with overblown strings and tons of syrupy melodies added by producer Ron Nevison. It has a country cinema vibe to it and is the complete opposite of what one might be expecting when hearing it for the first time. But lyrically it's deep and introspective...

They say that the night life

They say, it ain't no good life

But it's my life

I've been a gambler

I've been a thief

And most of my good friends

They don't hold with my belief

They say that the night life

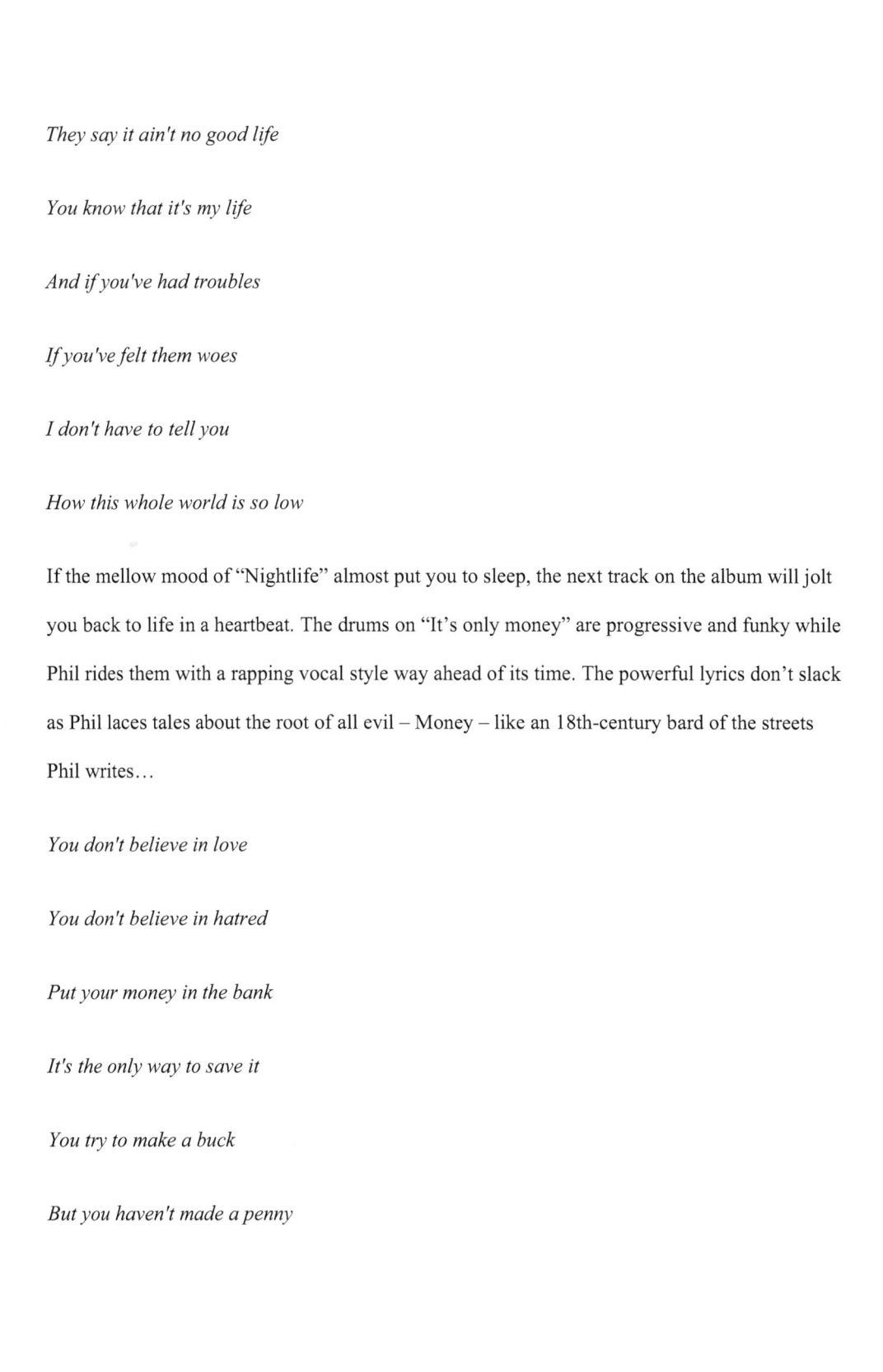

They say it ain't no good life

You know that it's my life

And if you've had troubles

If you've felt them woes

I don't have to tell you

How this whole world is so low

If the mellow mood of "Nightlife" almost put you to sleep, the next track on the album will jolt you back to life in a heartbeat. The drums on "It's only money" are progressive and funky while Phil rides them with a rapping vocal style way ahead of its time. The powerful lyrics don't slack as Phil laces tales about the root of all evil – Money – like an 18th-century bard of the streets Phil writes…

You don't believe in love

You don't believe in hatred

Put your money in the bank

It's the only way to save it

You try to make a buck

But you haven't made a penny

You need a little luck

But you know you won't get any

You don't believe in God

You don't believe in glory

You've got a brother in the clinic

Tells the same kind of story

If he had another life

He'd know what would be waiting

If he had another soul

He could sell it all to Satan

You don't believe in war

You don't believe in Jesus

Got a sister in New York

She knows how she pleases

Walking the streets

On the south side of the city

Trying to make ends meet

Isn't that a pity

She wants money

"Still in love with you" is probably the greatest ballad Thin Lizzy ever composed and recently enjoyed new appreciation thanks to the chart-topping cover by legendary British singer Sade. Like Phil, Sade is one of the few bi-racial singers to have crossover success in the UK and abroad. The definitive studio version of "Still in love" remains the one found on the Nightlife album. It's the only song that Phil and Brian recorded with Gary Moore during a spat of studio sessions in early 1974 that made it onto the album. It has the unmistakable Gary Moore sound that manages to set the tone perfectly for Phil's brokenhearted poetry.

Moore had been working out the melodies and arrangements for the song for about three years before entering the studio with Phil and Brian to record it. Gary didn't contribute much in the way of lyrics but when Phil felt the melancholy atmosphere of the guitar work he knew it had to be a delta blues break up song. When Robbo began plying the overdubs and rerecording the leads, he refused to play the solo, knowing that it would be impossible to improve upon Gary Moore's version. Although later on, Robbo would soon master and add his own flair to the "Still in love" solo, the Gary Moore version on the album Nightlife is one of the ultimate Lizzy musical highlights. The song also had an extra bit of vocal sauce added by the Scottish crooner

Frankie Miller, who sang duet and backup with Phil. The poetry is a simple, but it catches the morose mood of a breakup to perfection…

I think I'll fall to pieces

If I don't find something else to do

This sadness, it never ceases

Oh, I'm still in love with you

And my headache keeps on reeling

It's got me in a crazy spin

Darling, darling, darling is this the end?

They say time has a way of healing

Dries all the tears from your eyes

Darling, it's this empty feeling

That my heart can't disguise

After all that we've been through

I tried my best but it's no use

I guess I'll just keep loving you, is this the end?

Still in love with you

Now it's all over

There's something I think you should know

Baby, baby, think it over

Just one more time before you go

Call on me, baby

If there's anything I can do for you

Please call on me, baby

Help me see it through

"Frankie Carrol" is about a drunk that beats his kids and cheats on his wife. It sounds horrible, overblown on piano and strings and despite some honest and grimy storytelling the song is a dud. The sixth song on the album "Showdown" is funky as hell and has a great bassline accompanied by excellent snares, breaks and hi-hats by Brian. The guitar stabs are vintage Isaac Hayes and Robbo's solo shreds. Phil shows great range on the chorus and sings in a casual cool voice that feels like he's talking to you instead of singing. The song is about a showdown on the football field and Phil paints the picture of his favorite boot boy standing his ground for Manchester United, which was Phil's adopted football club in England way before they became a household name and one of the greatest sports franchises in the world. Once again, Phil demonstrates a profound understanding of the visual importance of the spoken word as he instantly teleports you to a dangerous soccer pitch in Britain.

Following "Showdown" is a short instrumental track called "Banshee" that adds another level of intrigue to the Nightlife album. It also makes you wonder why they didn't have more instrumentals on the rest of their albums. It certainly makes sense seeing that Lizzy was growing into a respected musical outfit. A poem named "Banshee" was discovered in one of Phil's early poetry books…

I was your lover

You were my queen

You broke my heart

I gave up everything

I was your friend

But you were my foe

I told you that

I could not let you go

At night I hear the wind calling

"Oh come back my darling"

Oh banshee! Oh banshee!

It keeps on calling me, keeps on calling me

We dance the night away

Oh we dance the night away

I won your heart

You took my soul

I love you then

But you left me cold

I was your lover

You were my queen

You broke my heart

I gave up everything

At night I can hear you calling

"Oh come back my darling"

Oh banshee! Oh banshee!

I hear you calling me, I hear you calling me

After the quirky instrumental the album's eighth track was the lead single "Philomena", a song Phil named after and wrote for his mother. It's a beautiful number that Phil sings in a heavy Irish accent and pours his heart into. He lifted the chorus of 'Home boys home' from an old Irish folk song "The Old country" and although those who left home to pursue their dreams can relate to it, it's rather a very deep and personal love letter from Phil to his mother…

I've been a wild wild rover

Sailed all over the sea

But this thing that makes me wonder

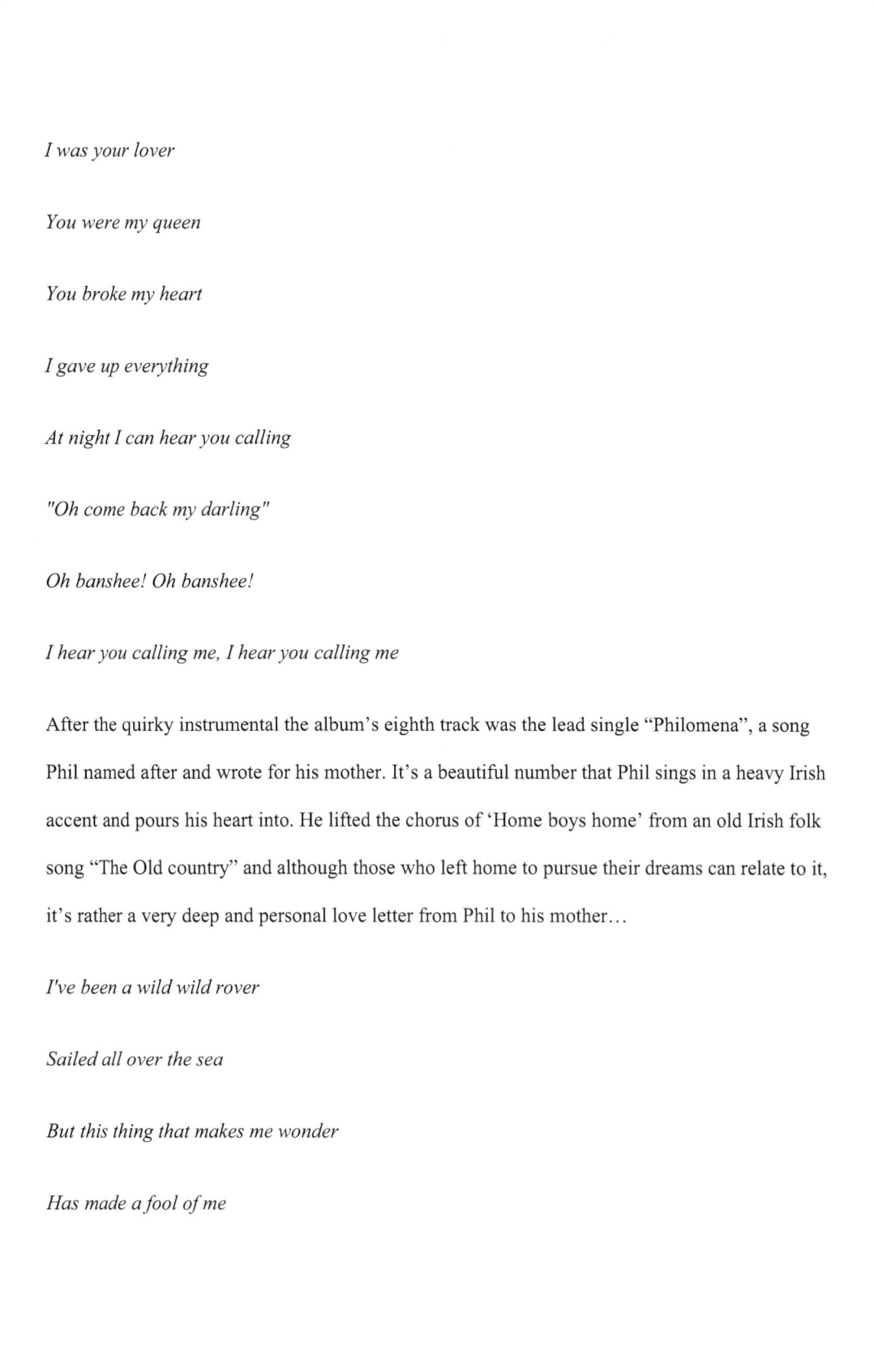

Has made a fool of me

For it took me from my childhood

Underneath the stars and skies

And I still hear the wind

Whistling through the wild wood, whispering goodbye

It's home boys home

She's home boys home

No matter

Where I roam

If you see my mother

Please give her all of my love

For she has a heart of gold there

As good as god above

If you see my mother

Tell her I'm keeping fine

Tell her that I love her

And I'll try and write sometime

"Sha-la-la" is a great sign of things to come for Thin Lizzy. It is by far the only song that rocks on Nightlife and is the first time that the twin guitar leads of Scott and Robbo produced good results. Brian's drumming approaches speed metal territory, unheard of in 1974 and he even kills a wicked solo halfway through the song. Brian Downey shines on this track. Phil's lyrics are pretty much throwaways for the awesome hook he created, which doesn't come in until after a great double guitar musical battle. The song ends with a scorching guitar solo and a fading drum solo. This song fucking rocks and contains shades of what the future had in store for Thin Lizzy. Unfortunately, the closing song on the album "Dear Heart" kills the rocking vibes set by "Sha-la-la" and should have been used earlier on in the album.

Knowing that they were working the kinks out with a new sound, Phil wasn't surprised when he learned that Nightlife flopped. He was hoping that the singles might fare better, but they didn't and the band placed most of the blame for the disappointing results on the soft touch of producer Ron Nevison. Phil was crushed that Vagabonds didn't take off and was unsure about what direction to musically head in, so he tried to make a soft rock countryish commercial sounding record. Stephen Thomas Erlewine of Allmusic writes:

It's curious that Night Life -- the first album Thin Lizzy recorded for Mercury, the first album to feature guitarists Scott Gorham and Brian Robertson, the album that in many ways kicked off their classic era -- is in many ways a complete anomaly within their catalog. It's a subdued, soulful record, smooth in ways that Thin Lizzy never were before and rarely were afterwards…There are still some moments of tough, primal rock & roll -- there's the funky workout of "It's Only Money" and the nasty "Sha-La-La," both excellent showcases for Gorham and Robertson -- but they stick out among the jazzy, soulful whole, even if they never quite disrupt the mood. And it's that mood that's so appealing about Night Life -- it's a warm, soulful sound that resonates in ways Thin Lizzy's earlier records didn't. And it's not just because of the feel of the music, either, it's due to Phil Lynott's increasing growth as a songwriter. [6]

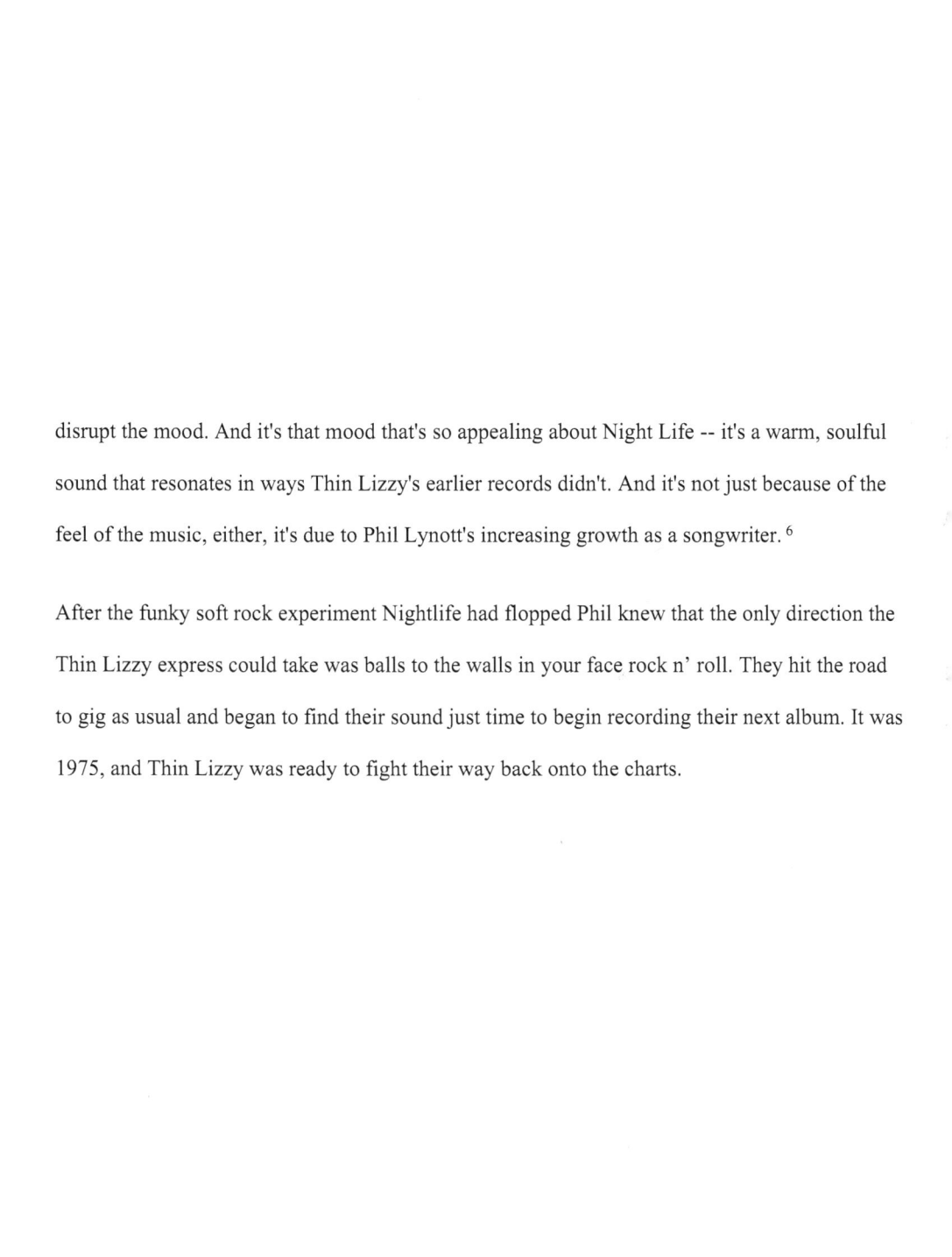

After the funky soft rock experiment Nightlife had flopped Phil knew that the only direction the Thin Lizzy express could take was balls to the walls in your face rock n' roll. They hit the road to gig as usual and began to find their sound just time to begin recording their next album. It was 1975, and Thin Lizzy was ready to fight their way back onto the charts.

Fighting!

Peace, re-assurance, pleasure, are the goals I seek

I cannot crawl one inch outside my proper skin

I talk of love --a scholar's parrot may talk Greek

But, self-imprisoned, always end where I begin

Only that now you have taught me (but how late) my lack

I see the chasm. And everything you are was making

My heart into a bridge by which I might get back

From exile, and grow man. And now the bridge is breaking

For this I bless you as the ruin falls. The pains

You give me are more precious than all other gains

C.S. Lewis

Already certified road warriors in Europe and the UK by March of 1975, Thin Lizzy finally toured the United States for the first time. For Phil, it was a mythical dream come true and he relished the thought of rocking America. Thin Lizzy would be supporting Bachman Turner Overdrive, ZZ Top, and Bob Seger on a six-week tour of the Midwest, and they couldn't have asked for better gatekeepers to introduce them to the American rock landscape. It was a big step up and Lizzy soon realized that rocking in America was a different beast altogether, this wasn't some one-horse town in Germany or a dive bar in Cork, this was fucking Elvis and the land of milk and honey.

With funds low and mostly spent on drinks, smoke, and cheeseburgers the boys were sleeping two to a bed in cheap hotels and living on the music. Thin Lizzy was a tight bunch of drinking misfits beginning to discover their sound. They were consuming gallons of alcohol and thought it to be no big deal when they took the stage thirty minutes late on their first show in Detroit, Michigan. A few nights later they repeated this practice in Louisville, Kentucky but the manager of BTO soon gave their lackadaisical ways a reality check. Scott Gorham remembers:

BTO were a very professional band, and gave us an indication of what was expected of us on a bigger stage. We went on that tour thinking that if we were supposed to be on at 8:00, we'd probably make it by about 8:30. That attitude ended the first night, when their manager had ours up against the wall by the scruff of his neck, threatening to throw us off the tour if we were ever late again. The next night we were on by 7:55! [7]

Thin Lizzy started to get serious after seeing the kind of dedication required to perform at the highest levels of the game. Night after night Phil and the boys watched Bob Seger, BTO and ZZ Top rock the shit out of audiences and began to realize what it took to be considered a world-class rock band. They became cool with Bob Seger especially Phil, who was impressed by Bob's songwriting skills and presence on stage. Phil found it odd that Bob wasn't playing his hit

"Rosalie" during his set, and made a little mental note to cover the song during an upcoming recording session. The six-week tour of the Midwest was a momentous gut check for Thin Lizzy, but they passed with flying colors. Although they had grown fond of spending time with Bob Seger, Lizzy had created beef with non-partying Mormon rockers BTO. Disgusted at Lizzy's tougher than nails lifestyle, BTO constantly clashed with them and to make matters worse, only a few weeks into the tour BTO began noticing that Lizzy had improved to the point of upstaging them every night. Robbo remembers:

Those fat Mormon shitheads. We were slim, fairly good looking and kicked their ass. We had a lot of angry episodes with them, Brian Downey especially. But they were Mormons for Christ sake – no sex, no drugs, no drink. And then Thin Lizzy happened along. They were convinced we were off our tits, which we were, but at the end of the night, when it came to playing we kicked their ass night after night.

Thin Lizzy was starting to get the hang of rocking in America and they weren't about to let BTO spoil their fun. They drank like sailors, went to strange bars in strange towns and fucked every American girl that they could. Robbo barely avoided jail when he smacked the shit out of a groupie that bit his tongue during a rough make out session. The irate groupie began screaming at and pushing Robbo all over the room to the dismay of Brian Downey, who was trying to watch the Ali-Frazier super fight on the room's television set. The groupie eventually left to Scott's room and then showed up at four in the morning with a police officer, claiming that she had been assaulted. Lizzy's managers diffused the situation with a bribe and Robbo was spared a police record in America.

The tour came to an end in late April, and the boys headed back to England with a newfound swagger. Inspired by the results and the feedback they received in America, they successfully rocked their homecoming gig at the Hammersmith Odeon on April 5th. Now supporting BTO on the European leg of the tour, Thin Lizzy was back on its home turf and confident of their new sound. Although BTO had a #1 hit in America with "You ain't seen nothing yet" they hadn't broke through to British audiences and Thin Lizzy knew BTO wasn't getting the same reaction from the crowds that they had been used to in the States. Robbo remembers opening for BTO:

We went on that tour with none of our own back line, hired gear and we still kicked their ass. After a few dates they asked us to headline and Phil politely declined with a wry smile…the one thing about being a support group is that you have nothing to lose. If you're the headliner and don't deliver the goods you're fucked. Phil realized that pretty early on and of course if the support band gave the headliner a run for the money all the reviews would be in our favor, Phil was very astute like that.

Thin Lizzy rocked with confidence yet unseen. The original Lizzy fans knew that a change had happened, and the group sounded tighter, smoother and better than ever before. Plus the twin guitar sound was evolving faster and sweeter sounding than anyone could have guessed. Thin Lizzy began to record their fifth album Fighting in the summer of 1975. Although never officially credited, Producer, Engineer, and Lizzy fan Keith Harwood, who helped out on Nightlife was brought in to assist the month long Thin Lizzy recording sessions at Olympic Studios in Barnes. Self-produced by Phil after the fiasco of Nightlife the boys took the bull by the horns and did everything their way while in the studio. During those recording sessions, Robbo and Scott finally gelled and established their unique twin guitar trademarked Thin Lizzy sound. It is evident as soon as you put the album on because Fighting sounds like nothing at all compared with the band's first four albums. This is when the official Thin Lizzy era begins. Fighting is unmistakable and distinctive, signaling that the boys had finally found their musical pathway, even though the album still had its fair amount of flaws. When they turned the masters in to head A&R Nigel Grainge, he called them back the next day and told them to get rid of four tracks and come back with four better ones.

Nigel was expecting to be told to go "Fuck off!" by the hardcore rockers - after all Thin Lizzy was the most feared band within the offices of Vertigo. But Nigel was shocked when instead of making a stink, Phil asked him asked for advice. Phil was a tough rocking dude on the outside, but inside he truly was a sensitive poet who cared about what people thought of the music. After discussing some ideas Phil was given an extra $10,000 to head back to the Olympic and come up with four new songs, one of which was the spectacular piece he co-wrote with Scott "King's Vengeance".

With the album turned now in Vertigo's hands it was time once again to hit the road in support of their leadoff single, the Bob Seger cover "Rosalie". Originally released on Bob Seger's 1973 album Back in '72 "Rosalie" was inspired by Bob's crush on a Canadian DJ and hit the charts as a 7" single in the UK and USA. Thin Lizzy speeded up the tempo and added their distinct flair to the track, making it their very own. In fact over the years most people would soon forget the Bob Seger version, as "Rosalie" became such a fan favorite and set list staple of Thin Lizzy's future shows. Surprisingly "Rosalie" failed to chart but thirty years later this 45 has become one of the great singles sought by record collectors and Lizzy aficionados. Mostly because of the fabulous anti-racist reggae B-side "Half-Caste" which was recently made available for the first time since

1975, when the Fighting album was released as a Deluxe Edition in 2012. Phil's lyrics aren't shy about his feelings on race and by issuing it as a B-side he wanted to drive the point home and make it clear to all that racism is old fashioned and extremely lame…

I got a girl in Brixton town

Her daddy don't like me hangin' 'round

The boy ain't black, the boy is brown

Don't he know it's a halfcaste town

I got a girl up near Richmond way

Her daddy don't want me to lead the girl astray

The brown boy is born to serve he say

Don't he know it's a different day

Embarking on a mammoth British tour Thin Lizzy's insane amount of roadwork was finally paying off. The crowds were bigger and jaws dropping at the sound and fury coming out of the amplifiers. The Thin Lizzy train was finally on the right track and moving full steam ahead. When they reported back to the Vertigo offices to discuss album cover ideas, the suits at Vertigo decided not to go for another Fitzpatrick art piece. They claimed that Lizzy was lacking an image and decided to give them one with iron pipes, bats and knives. Phil rejected the idea because he knew that they were serious musicians and the last thing they wanted to be considered was a thug band. His opinion went unheard and the boys were assigned photographers and driven to a rough and grimy back alley in London.

Although the cover is unfavorably considered one of the corniest in rock history it shouldn't be, because the image of a thuggish ruggish Thin Lizzy, each strapped with a bat, iron pipe and knife, waiting to kick ass in some dark alley has become iconic. The album cover even helped inspire the punk movement and despite Robbo's opinion that it is the, "Worse cover to grace an album sleeve" it is in fact absolutely brilliant! Not only does it reflect accurately the type of sound and image future generations would attach to Lizzy, but also it's so fucking hard and scary that for the rest of their careers they didn't have to worry about doing another group picture album cover again.

The band's fifth album Fighting was released on September 12th, 1975 and is the only album to feature the official Thin Lizzy logo designed by Fitzpatrick. By the 27th, Fighting became the first Lizzy album to chart in Britain reaching #60 and selling a reported 20,000 copies. After four albums of trying to find themselves and their sound, Phil and Brian finally discovered the answer with the addition of Scott and Robbo whose harmonizing guitar interplay provided the missing pieces of the puzzle. Fighting has the key elements of hard rock, pop, blues and progressive twin guitar melodies that would come to define their future albums.

The beauty of the album is how easy it is to listen to and despite the punky album cover Fighting will not make your ears bleed. The guitars don't screech, they harmonize and Phil's vocals aren't screamed they're crooned to perfection. Aided by the drum and bass work that fits together like a reggae outfit, the album is dark in places and fluffy in others but balanced enough to make you wanna pick a fight but then after getting your nose bloody, ponder deeply about life, death and social injustices.

The vibe of the album is classic rock n' roll and once you start listening to it the fears the album cover may have instilled in you quickly disappear. Even though Thin Lizzy could definitely drink all your booze, steal your chick and kick your ass all in quick succession they could also shock you by writing and performing music on a Beethoven-Lord Byron-esque level higher than most would have expected based off their appearance. After "Rosalie" opens the album, it is successfully followed by the Phil Lynott original "For those who love to live" a song inspired by the life of football legend George Best. Phil and George became friends and drinking buddies after Phil's mother opened a small hotel in Manchester. George loved to drink at the quiet hotel and Phil and the boys always came to visit whenever they were in the area, producing a long lasting friendship.

Phil loved football and if he weren't such a gifted artist most likely would have chosen football as his main occupation, at one point Phil even bought shares in the Manchester United football club, an investment that would have made him millions if he had lived long enough. Phil wouldn't miss a match and sometimes even pushed gigs back until the contest ended, his love of football made him more than qualified to write a song about young lads dreaming of gold medals and green pitches far beyond their impoverished home turf. Phil writes…

You've got to give a little love

To those who love to live

You've got to take a little hate

From those who have to wait

The album's next track "Suicide" was originally performed as "Baby's been Messing" during the Eric Bell era and can be heard in a rough version on the BBC broadcast from July of 1973. Robbo and Scott give it a hard blues sound both progressive and electric without going overboard. With a great drum breakdown and dueling solos "Suicide" would go on to be another Lizzy live set favorite. In a Swedish fan club interview from 1981 Phil talks about the songs origins:

Suicide is the oldest number in the set. Suicide we did even as a three piece band. There's a version of that, that they have at Decca Records and I won't let them release that…It was written '71, '72. #81 was funny 'cos #81 was the number of the bus that I used to get home.

Referenced in the song #81 of course was assigned to the John Doe who committed suicide. The next song on the album "Wild one" is a true Thin Lizzy classic. Released as the lead single on October 17th, it's almost unbelievable that the song failed to chart. Beautifully arranged with lush guitars cascading all over each other in harmonic complexities Wishbone Ash could only dream of creating, "Wild one" isn't a love song and one can interpret it many ways. To most listeners the song seems to be about the worried heart of a father that finally sees the day when his only daughter leaves home. Phil wrote "Wild one" and related it to all the people that had left Ireland to forge better lives for themselves:

I was just thinking generally about people who had left the country. Anybody that was hip. Like, there's an awful lot of really clever Irish people in London, right? The amount of Irish guys there hustling on the King's Road is great. And they're all deluxe hustlers. Only the cream go away and survive in London. I just thought that in the song it was a terrible waste of talent. The song is really very simple. The lyrics are really very simple. 'You go your way and I'll try to follow, and if you change your mind I will be waiting for you here tomorrow.' All the time 'I' is supposed to represent Ireland. The call of Ireland to its wild ones to come back. That was the idea, but I put it in such a way that it came across as if it was a love song. [8]

Phil's "simple" idea and "simple" lyrics are truly amazing especially when complimented by a band that finally found their niche…

Wild one

The gypsies warned of the danger

You can laugh and joke with friends

But don't you ever talk to strangers

Although their offers may be sweet

And I'd bet and I would wager

Away you'll stray and never come back

To those who love and made you

The album's fifth cut "Fighting my way back" rocks hard and does the album cover justice. It makes you want to kick somebody's ass but also has a great message about not being a puppet, to get up, brush yourself off and be a better person looking to a brighter future - if you can. It's brutally honest and inspiring, with a monster hook, angry guitars and drum work that stands the test of time. Easily could be featured in any movie requiring an inspirational montage scene. It was actually inspired by the pressure that Phil was facing from the record company to produce another hit…

Well, I'm tough, rough, ready and I'm able

To pick myself up from under this table

Don't just stick no sign on me, I got no label

I'm a little sick, unsure, unsound and unstable

But, I'm fighting my way back

Well, I'm busting out and I'm going in

And I'm kickin' up about the state I'm in

Looking to my future, not my past

I want to be a good boy, but how long can it last?

"King's Vengeance" is an epic tale set in the middle ages or so it feels like. Co-written by Scott Gorham who adds his warm laid back feel and acoustics, it's a curious song about a springtime death a commoner was facing. Awaiting the wrath of the King's justice for some petty offense, the song is an ode to the working class fan base that Lizzy was rooted in. It's a marvelous bit of storytelling about the plight of the poor season after season…

Spring she comes and spring she teases

Brings summer winds and summer breezes

Blow through your hair till autumn leaves us

When autumn leaves us, oh how winter freezes

And the child is still breathing

With the beating of a heart (with the beating of the heart)

Some say we are equal

Some a million miles apart

Maybe the commoner got beheaded? That's exactly the feel you get as "King's Vengeance" fades out in a fuzzy guitar echo and blends simultaneously into the haunting "Spirit Slips Away" a chilling and desolate song about the mysteries of death. The drums are sparse and the guitars distorted, heavy and impressive, especially Robbo's mournful solo. The bass line moves like a funeral precession and Phil sings with sad passion and disillusioned emotion, questioning death like it weighed heavily on his mind. The morbid atmosphere of the song is captured perfectly all the way up until the ending when the song fades out with chilling wind effects. You feel like you're standing in an ancient cemetery…

May the angels bring their flame to you

When your spirit slips away

And when the music that makes you blue

Unfolds its secrets, the mysteries are told to you

May the angels sing rejoice to you

That fateful day when your spirit slips away

Unfortunately after this song the "Fighting" album loses steam and stutters to its end with three tracks that are barely worth mentioning. "Silver dollar" the first song written by Robbo and "Ballad of a hard man" a Scott Gorham clunker along with the clichéd "Freedom song" by Phil round out the album and kill whatever momentum the first seven songs had going for them.

Once again, Stephen Thomas Erlewine follows up his review of Lizzy's fourth album Nightlife with a review of their fifth Fighting for Allmusic:

It's hard not to interpret the "fighting my way back" chorus of the title track on Thin Lizzy's fifth album as the band's way of bouncing back from the uncommonly subdued Night Life. If that record was smooth and relaxed, Fighting is a tense, coiled, vicious rock & roll album, as hard as Vagabonds' toughest moments but more accomplished, the sound of a band truly coming into its own. There are two key forces at work. First, there's the integration of guitarists Scott Gorham and Brian Robertson, who get to unleash furious playing on every track here. It's hard not to thrill at their harmonizing twin-lead interplay, which is enough to excuse the rather pedestrian nature of their original tunes here (Robertson penned the boogie "Silver Dollar," Gorham the closer "Ballad of a Hard Man"). That's especially true because of the other development here: the full flourishing of Phil Lynott as a rock & roll poet. Strangely enough, that leap forward as a writer is somewhat overshadowed by a triumph of the band, in how they completely steal Bob Seger's "Rosalie" turning it into their own anthem, but that again is a testament to the strength of this incarnation of Thin Lizzy, who truly begin their classic era with this dynamic LP. [9]

Rejected Artwork

Although Fighting had charted, it was still considered a flop and its two singles also failed to make a dent. Despite not selling a lot of albums, by the end of 1975 Lizzy had earned stripes as the hardest working, take no shit, musically diverse rock band in the business. Phil and the boys could feel that 1976 was going to be a big year for them. The record label hoped so because Lizzy's first two albums and accompanying singles had left them in the red. Thin Lizzy was in debt and more specifically Phil was in the same position he was in before "Whiskey in a jar" blew up. Once again told by record label heads that it's make it or break it time boys and if Lizzy didn't deliver a hit on the next album, their days with Vertigo were over. Phil looked to the States hoping to write an American sounding rock song that would finally put Thin Lizzy on the map. All he needed was a little inspiration, which he found after watching a program about young soldiers returning home from the war in Vietnam.

G.I. Joe is back in Town

The land to whelm -- which fires the orb of noon

And fills the crescent of the milder moon

Who'st meted forth alternate day and night

And numbered all the stars -- their places bright

Their signs, times, courses only known to Thee

Who hast to many forms, most wondrously

The new earth shaped, and given to dead dust life

Who hast lost Man restored, for fruit of strife

So ancient Faith attests, so tell the hours

No time can change, no age abate Thy powers!

Whereof to sing, in little part, afraid I seek, as entering a great forest-glade

One strives an over-arching bough to reach

What were an hundred tongues, an iron speech

Or what were man an hundredfold to show

Things more than all the lucid stars that glow

And all the sands where all the oceans flow!

Caelius Sedulius

Thin Lizzy feverishly out rocked their supporting acts Bad Company, Nazareth and Status Quo, closing out 1975 in an epic New Year's Eve show that had Hammersmith Street buzzing. Thin Lizzy's first two albums for Vertigo and their accompanying singles had bombed but it was due to the strength of their live shows and Fighting's ability to sneak onto the charts that kept them barely above the trash heap of ordinary. Lizzy's audience of die-hard fans was still there but the big league breakthrough eluded them. For Phil the night he rocked the Top of the Pops seemed like a million years ago. With the pressure at an all-time peak the boys were obligated to enter the recording studios in early January to begin work on their sixth album with the hopes of finally delivering the goods.

Disappointed that their self-produced album Fighting hadn't turned out sounding like they expected and still reeling from the Nightlife fiasco, Phil sent word seeking help with turning their live sound into a worthy translation inside the studio. Former The Who producer and engineer John Alcock was at the top of their list and they made the drive to see them on a gray, stormy night typically seen during a horrible English winter. After meeting Phil and the boys, it was decided to begin production immediately at Alcock's Ramport Studios deep in Battersea's countryside. The inspiring studio was shaded by trees, pastures and rolling green hills. When Thin Lizzy arrived in the heart of winter they had plenty of time to write, rehearse and focus on making a top shelf commercially viable album. But as the cold weeks stretched on rehearsals didn't go very well, Alcock was having difficulties getting the sound together and the heat from vertigo was intense.

With little money and no turning back the pressure to produce a hit was starting to become unbearable for Phil. Despite having his back against the wall, creatively he was in the zone writing like a mad man knowing this was his last shot at hitting the big time. Working among farmlands in the middle of nowhere, by February Thin Lizzy's sonic output was beginning to come together and the American sound Alcock was aiming for was being manifested in the studio. Alcock, already an accomplished producer began to harness and use the varying strengths of Lizzy's twin guitarists. Alcock discovered that Robbo was an emotional player, and his lightning in the bottle style had to be captured when it poured out naturally. Scott was more of a technical player and was easier to instruct and had good instincts of what should be played and where. Alcock was impressed by Lizzy's development during the album's recording but still made improvements towards making a more commercial sounding album by going to extra lengths that infuriated Robbo by bringing in session players. Thin Lizzy worked 15 to 18 hours a day for 5 straight weeks in Battersea until finishing their sixth album Jailbreak.

With their new album complete it was back on the road for the rock warriors who relentlessly toured while the album was being mastered and assembled at Vertigo. With no idea of what the lead single should be Phil figured that "Running Back" would be given the green light but was enthusiastically told by the suits that his ode to soldiers returning home from Vietnam "G. I. Joe is back" had set the offices of Mercury Records in America on fire. Phil changed the title to the simply brilliant "The Boys are back in town" and a song that almost didn't make the album was destined to launch Thin Lizzy to worldwide fame and fortune.

Vertigo planned the launch for the album in Dublin's Tara Hotel and afterward the party continued down the street at McNeary's pub off Grafton Street with drinks spiked with acid. They barely had time to get their shit together before being rushed off to America for a six-week supporting tour of ZZ Top, Aerosmith, Reo Speedwagon, Rush and Styx. Back in America Phil, and the boys were unaware of the massive buzz that began to generate within the walls of Vertigo's American subsidiary label Mercury Records. The American suits instinctively knew Jailbreak was the goods and went all in with a shrewd move by deciding to release "The Boys are back" as the lead single in America. To the shock of everyone it blew the fuck up and peaked at #12 on the Billboard music charts. Thin Lizzy had finally arrived and after only a few weeks of supporting Aerosmith they now commanded their own headlining tour. After nearly a decade of performing together Phil and Brian finally were bona fide rock stars as "The Boys" stormed the charts on both sides of the Atlantic and shot to #8 on the English charts and #1 naturally in Ireland, but the biggest jolt of all was that their sixth album Jailbreak had landed at #18 on the Billboard top 200 in America and #10 in the UK. Thanks to America, the Jailbreak album made Thin Lizzy stars and put them on the map.

Decades later it's still a cherished rock album in the States and while most Americans might not even know that Thin Lizzy was an Irish rock group they certainly would recognize the iconic album cover masterfully designed by Jim Fitzpatrick. The Jailbreak cover has an awesome Marvel-esque comic art style illustrating Thin Lizzy busting out of a totalitarian prison in one of the greatest and most recognizable album covers in American rock history. It has been a staple of teenage boys' bedrooms from generation to generation and decades after your first notice of it possibly on an 8 track tape in your uncle's truck it still resonates with the same epic force when seeing it lit up in your Itunes display window. Now bona fide rock stars Thin Lizzy's gig fee dramatically rose from $500 a show to $5,000 and soon Phil flew his mother Philomena over to join them on their tour of America. With fancy limousines, and five star hotel employees waiting on them hand and feet, Philomena was immensely proud of Phil and the boys as she enjoyed a great time far removed from the abject poverty they had grown up in. Lizzy mania swept up and down America and after a triumphant showing on the popular late night television program Don Kirshner's Rock Concert Lizzy's audience grew from 600 people a show to over 6,000 waiting to be rocked. And with a chart smashing album and newfound acceptance into the close-knit rock royalty circles Thin Lizzy wasted no time adjusting to living the life of rock gods.

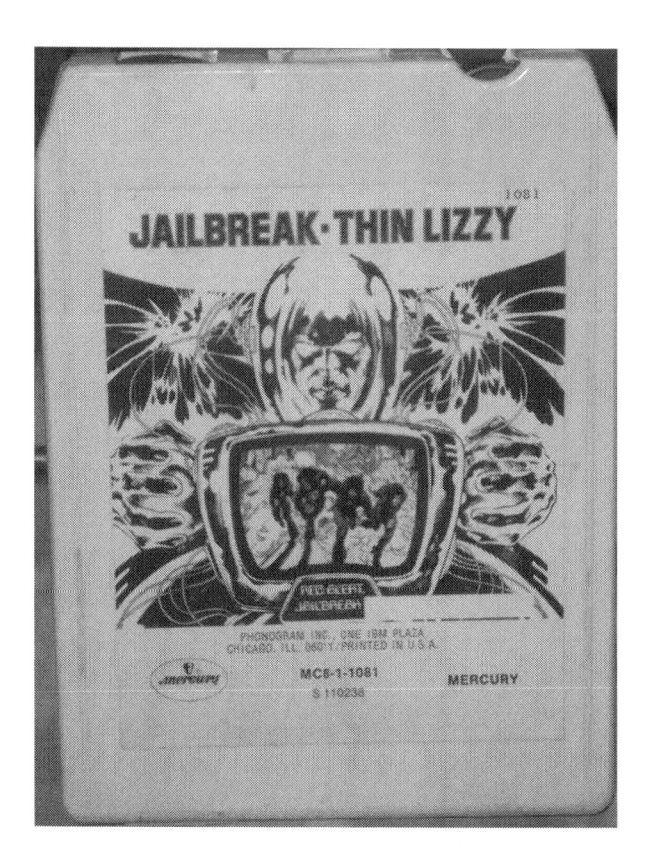

With its sci-fi cover and accompanying story found on the back side of the album Jailbreak appeared to be an epic concept album in the fashion of the Who's Quadrophenia and David Bowie's Diamond Dogs, but despite a few linking passages found in Phil's lyrics the album's title track is the only theme that can be associated with the album cover. It would have been an extra treat if Phil decided to conceive a concept album with Fitzpatrick's cover in mind, but

Jailbreak is not a traditional concept album if one at all. Or is it? Whatever Lizzy's original intentions were Jailbreak has evolved into one of the finest examples of a rock album that managed to capture the sound of an era so perfectly that it is universally recognized as one of the true gems recorded in the 1970's. Kicking off with the prison escaping title track "Jailbreak" the album's powerful introduction grabs you by the balls and throws you up against the wall. With the opening guitar fuzz and sirens echoing through the speakers, an unmistakable force thrusts its sound upon the listener and demands that it be heard. With incredible story telling lyrics from Phil and a melodic twin guitar harmony sprinkled with Robbo's wah wah effects and Brian's snappy shaker engulfed drumming, "Jailbreak" is easily one of Thin Lizzy's best songs ever. Phil's vocals capture the vibe of the song to eerie perfection and he delivers a performance with so much swag that it has transcended the ages as a classic vocal performance. It's also a benchmark in lyrical storytelling used in a rock song…

Tonight there's gonna be a jailbreak

Somewhere in this town

See me and the boys we don't like it

So were getting up and going down

Hiding low, looking right to left

If you see us coming, I think it's best

To move away, do you hear what I say?

From under my breath

Tonight there's gonna be a jailbreak

Somewhere in the town

Tonight there's gonna be a jailbreak

So don't you be around

Tonight there's gonna be trouble

Some of us won't survive

See the boys and me, we mean business

Bustin' out dead or alive

I can hear the hound dogs on my trail

All hell breaks loose, alarm and sirens wail

Like the game if you lose

Go to jail

Tonight there's gonna be a breakout

Into the city zones

Don't you dare to try and stop us

No one could for long

Searchlight on my trail

Tonight's the night, all systems fail

Hey you, good lookin' female

Come here

After having successfully busted out of prison the boys find themselves on the cool shores of the California coast where Phil's pen was clearly intent on painting a specific view of how he saw the mythical lands of America. The album's second song "Angel of the Coast" has the warm vibes of a Doobie Brothers song and funky west coast acoustic riffs with jazzy funked up drums. It follows the lyrical storytelling style of the first song and is another Lynott penned gem about a junkie that barely escapes a mob killing…

The sacred heart is bleeding

Go tell the Holy Ghost

That the junkie is still cheating

To get the thing he needs the most

Lady Luck has got me covered

Keeping her watchful eyes over me

The lovers are discovered

The charge is first degree

Angel, she's a killer

She's just flown in from the coast

Makes the hit, it's a winner

Leaves you dead as the post

Then Sally took to playing poker

The joker is her favorite card

And the drunk he can't stay sober

He says it's oh, much too hard, it's much too hard

Meantime something seedy

Was happening across the hall

Someone seemed to be groaning

You could hear it through the wall

And the cops they came like lightning

The bullets flew astray

And the noise it was frightening

But the crook he got away

The third song on the Jailbreak album "Running back" has an instantly recognizable riff that Robbo never got enough credit for. With sweet horns, a subtle groove and impressive crooning from Phil it's another standout yet overlooked track on the album that Phil admits was totally inspired by the years spent listening to Van Morrison. When asked by New Musical Express on November 6th, 1976 "Who first turned you on to rock when you were a kid?" Phil responded, "Van Morrison, the song 'Running Back' is very much influenced by Van. I really like that song. I used to go to Van's gigs in Ireland. He was the one who was happening in England, he was with Them at the time."

Although simple, "Running back" is another testament to Phil's songwriting ability…

I'm a fool now that it's over

Can you guess my name?

I make my money singing songs about you

It's my claim to fame

When they say it's over

It's not all over, there's still the pain

And I'd come running

I'd come running back to you again

Oh, I'd come running

I'd come running back to you again

If I said I was sorry

Would you still leave me?

I never thought you'd go 'till you did

Believe me

When they say it's over

It's not all over completely'

Cause I'd come running

I'd come running back to you again

The pace of the album chugs full steam ahead with the album's fourth song "Romeo and the Lonely Girl" a spectacular songwriting jewel penned by Phil about the insecurities and complexities of being a failed Romeo…

Romeo he had it rough

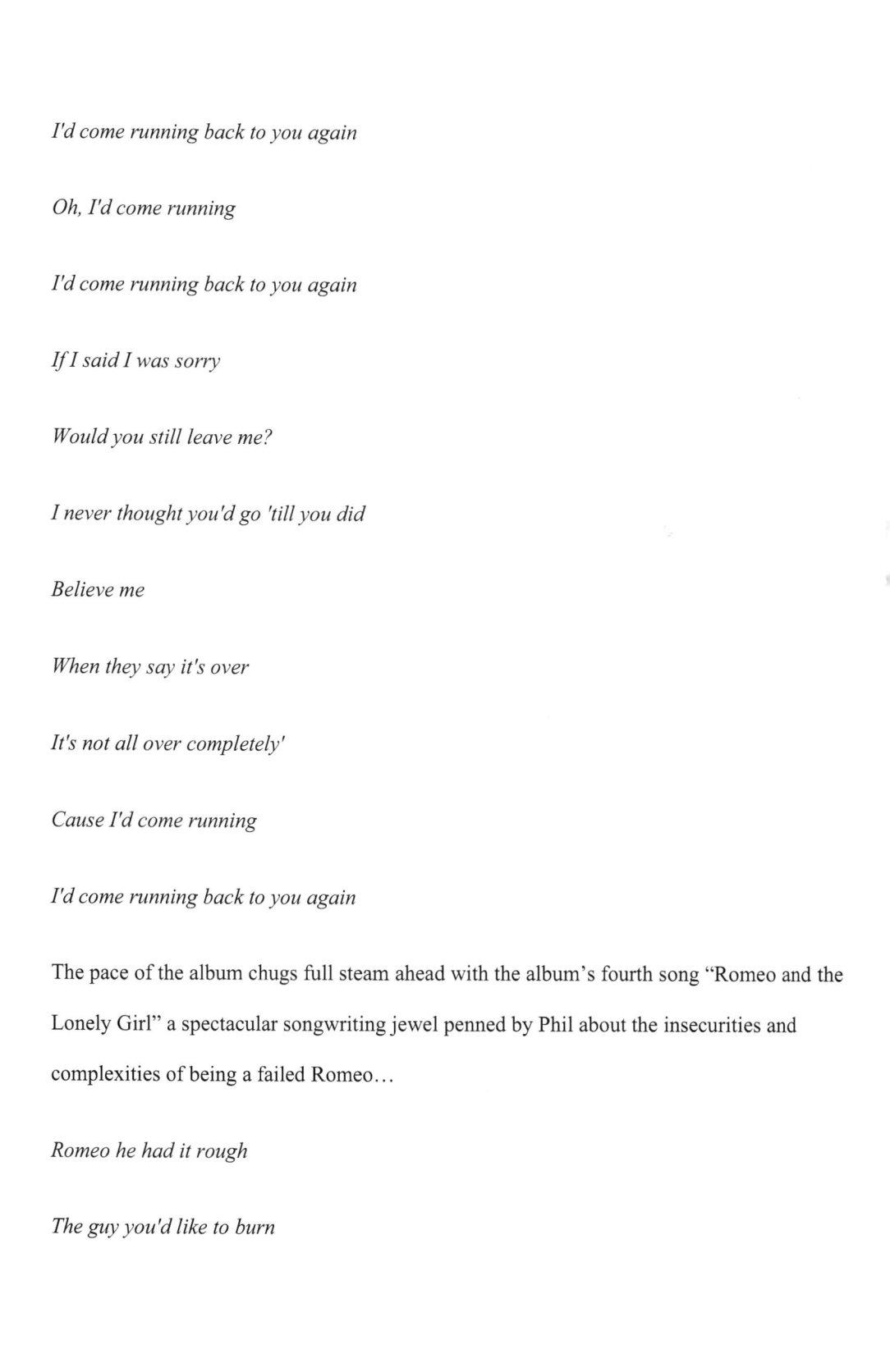

The guy you'd like to burn

But everything that Romeo had

You can bet it was well earned

For all his good looks there were scars that he took

And a lesson to be learned

Never judge lovers by a good looking covers

The lover might be spurned

The album's fifth song returns to its hard rocking roots with the superb "Warriors". A cut inspired by the sudden deaths of the great guitarists Jimi Hendrix and Duane Allman. With a thumping intro of dueling guitar pans and an epic sweeping bass line, the drums rattle while Phil's vocals run through a phaser chamber that pumps out his poetry in a sonic melting of echoes. A blistering solo by Robbo, hammering drums by Brian and a lush angelic arrangement of choir harmonies cement the track as an all-time hard rocking Lizzy classic.

The second half of the album kicks off with the unmistakable chart assaulting "The Boys Are Back in Town" a song that has become such a mainstream staple to the point of annoyance to its surviving creators. In America, it even appears in a Chase bank commercial! Despite the corny sugar coating and the much-deserved commercial popularity, it is without doubt one of the top five greatest songs ever written about rock n' roll and has secured Thin Lizzy a spot on its sacred list of immortality. The song was the summertime smash of 1976 and a brilliant example of how a band could present a powerful rock tune to the mainstream without losing any credibility. Containing some fantastic passing chords and changes, sweet guitar melodies, Phil's macho bravado and a monster hook, it ranks high on the all-time hits chart and is usually one of the first songs taught to aspiring teenage rockers...

Guess who just got back today?

Those wild eyed boys that've been away

Haven't changed, haven't much to say

But man I still think them cats are crazy

They were askin' if you were around

How you was where you could be found?

Told 'em you were livin' downtown

Driving all the old men crazy

Scott explains how Thin Lizzy's most famous song almost never was:

It was one of the 16 or 18 songs we recorded for the 'Jailbreak' album. At that time we needed to decide what tracks would be on the album and what ones we would skip. We loved this song but at that time we had doubts whether we would put it on the album or not. I personally thought the lyrics were better than the music. Phil did a great job. Then our manager decided this was a fantastic song and definitely should be on the album, we all consented. The rest is history, it was a top 5 hit in the US and made the 'Jailbreak' album platinum. Sometimes you're so closely involved with writing songs you can't give an objective opinion about them anymore, you can't see the strong points and the weak spots anymore. You need someone outside the band to give their perspective, but anyway I'm very happy the song made the album![10]

"The Boys" gave Lizzy the break they desperately needed and manifested them into a top ten band worthy of the accolade. It is a song that every street gang in the world could identify with, a ballsy rock anthem with no chicks involved, only lads out for a night on the town, cruising for a bruising, getting smashed on Friday night and going to the football match with a hangover the next day. Phil wrote the song without a proper hook and it almost drove him mad knowing that he had a great bunch of lyrics without the support of a strong chorus. He recalls:

I had most of the lyrics done to that for ages and I couldn't get the hook line, I couldn't get 'The Boys Are Back In Town' line and yet it sounds really natural, I was callin' it 'G.I. Joe is Back', 'The kids are back in town' and then I thought it was like 'The Who', you know, 'The kid's are allright' And you'd think that 'The Boys...' would come to me, it wouldn't but I couldn't think…I knew it had to be someone back in town and I was goin' around for about a week just waiting, and I knew when it'd come to me it'd be right but I couldn't think it. I was wreckin' me brains. It was a case of overthinkin' and somebody said to me one day, "The boys are playin' at such and such." That's it!! I just went mad in front of this guy and he's going "Wha??!!" I'm just going mad, it's OK. That was the 'Boys Are Back in Town'. That was the word I was looking for.

Of course following such a classic track like "The Boys" is almost impossible and the album's seventh track "Fight or Fall" obviously pales in comparison. The weakest track on the album, the song still has some good things going for it including Phil's lovely singing and a smooth laid back solo from Scott, but overall loses its edge halfway through and is the first song on the album that fails to hold the listener's attention. The album's next song grabs a hold of you instantly and has gone on to become another one of Lizzy's most cherished tunes.

Painting the picture of the American West like no other song before or since, Phil Lynott's masterful ode to the Pioneering spirit "Cowboy Song" is perhaps the best song on the Jailbreak album. It grew to be a popular set list staple where future crowds ended up singing the song back to a delighted Phil during performances. Scott remembers when Phil wrote the song after an inspiring visit to Texas:

We just ended the US tour and everyone had fallen in love with Texas, especially Phil, who went bezerk in Dallas and Houston. When the tour ended we went straight to the recording studio and Phil wrote 'Cowboy Song'. I think it was a salute to the Texas audience because they've given us such a great welcome. I thought it was awesome, since I'm an American and never had been in Texas before. The first time we toured in the US was also the first time for me I visited several States. I'm from California and I remember when we arrived in New York for the first time The band asked me 'Ok, this is your country, where can we go for a beer in New York?' I didn't know, I had never been there. [11]

"Cowboy Song" is one of Phil's best vocal performances and he croons slowly in the songs opener like the Irish singer Frankie Miller. It is an epic song, overall the longest one on the album and it features great guitar work and tempo swings. For a brief time it was called "Derby Blues" and even appeared on their live sets before the polished studio version was recorded. Phil's lyrics put you on the range…

I am just a cowboy lonesome on the trail

A starry night, a campfire light

The coyote call, the howling winds wail

So I ride out to the old sundown

I am just a cowboy lonesome on the trail

Lord, I'm just thinking about a certain female

The album closes with the epic "Emerald" a hammering tune full of Irish imagery, mysticism and archaic history. On an album that had been an experiment to capture the American sound, Phil closed it with a tale of conquest set in Ireland. Phil was a proud Irishman and was well aware of all the Irish families that had immigrated to America. Phil lifted the songs opening line from the Irish folk tale "McAlpine's Fusiliers" which goes "As down the glen came McAlpine's men, with their shovels slung behind them…"

Sounds magazine described "Emerald" in an issue released on April 14, 1979:

But watch them on a song like 'Emerald' when Lynott becomes the warrior leading a mighty avenging army and out in front of a couple of thousand hands flash skywards volunteering to leave homes, families and shit hole jobs and sign up in some volunteer force that'll rid the world of evil: that is Lizzy, no answers, no alternatives, just plain old fashioned Rock dream. [12]

Indeed as Phil's mighty lyrics demonstrate…

Down from the glen came the marching men

With their shields and their swords

To fight the fight they believed to be right

Overthrow the overlords

To the town where there was plenty

They brought plunder, swords and flame

When they left the town was empty

Children would never play again

"Emerald" is one of Lizzy's most recognizable and loved tracks and remained in the live set right until the very end, a scorcher that features some iconic guitar dueling, crunching drum work and some menacing yet heartfelt vocals from Phil. It is without a doubt the finest example of the trademarked Robbo and Scott Thin Lizzy double axe sound attack, and a powerful way to end a classic album. Thin Lizzy was now the toast of the American rock circuit and the first British band to make an impact there in 1976.

While Jailbreak is now universally recognized as a classic rock album, the momentum it was carrying for the boys during its release in America was brought to a screeching halt during a night of thunderstorms and terrible rainy weather. Phil turned pale, his eyes shaded yellow and his plague like appearance left him quarantined in a hospital in Columbus, Ohio. He was stricken with Hepatitis-C and languished near death for nearly a week as the tour was canceled to the disappointment of the band. The boys were on fire musically and publicly they had been able to cross over to the mainstream resulting in packed houses and commercial airtime. They were about to get a helluva lot bigger with the announcement of them joining Ritchie Blackmore's Rainbow tour as the supporting act. But before the tour ever got started Phil got sick and their tour of America officially ended. The luck of the Irish abandoned them and the Thin Lizzy express had been halted in its tracks thanks to Hepatitis-C.

The boys flew back to London and Phil rested and recuperated at his mother's hotel in Manchester. He watched football matches and replenished his health slowly. By July 11th, he felt good enough to join the boys as Thin Lizzy rocked a one night engagement at the Hammersmith Odeon. By the end of the month "Jailbreak" had been released as a single and Phil finally made it back to the Top of the Pops, but the experience wasn't what the boys were expecting and none of them held the moment with high regard. It was a disaster, and highly strange because it was the day that Phil's father showed up to meet him. Phil didn't respond very well to the weird encounter and making matters worse the gear and recording set up was backward. Robbo recalled:

The BBC are fucked up. Everything to do with them is a joke. The first ever session we did for the BBC, we walked in this particular day which also happened to be the day that Phil's dad turned up. The mixing desk was backwards and the faders were the same. It is so institutionalized, they're horrendously crap. [13]

Their performance was also crap, mostly because Phil was bugged out from meeting his biological father who had abandoned him, plus he still hadn't fully recovered after getting sick, and the usually tight band hadn't rehearsed or played together for almost two months. Truthfully they were exhausted and still floating from the sudden rush of fame in America. Despite the music not sounding as good as it should have, esthetically Thin Lizzy looked fabulous and Phil's cool macho posturing with eyes hidden beneath shaded aviator sunglasses has become iconic. New generations of English kids watching at home on the BBC were introduced to the Thin Lizzy sound that they would help popularize and keep cool for generations to come.

With legitimate success and a huge boulder finally lifted off Phil's shoulders thanks to "The Boys" becoming a top ten hit, it was time to relax and kick up their feet. They had been touring nonstop for almost seven years straight and the lull after the American tour was one of their longest breaks ever. They needed the time to recharge the Lizzy battery, and as Phil slowly recovered from his battle with the C monster, he began writing at a furious pace during the downtime. Producer John Alcock recognized this and immediately booked Thin Lizzy to begin work on their seventh album at the famously haunted Musicland recording studio deep in the heart of East Munich. While in Germany Phil would do some of his best writing, the boys would do some of their best playing and Johnny the Fox looked for Jimmy the Weed down on 1st Street and Main.

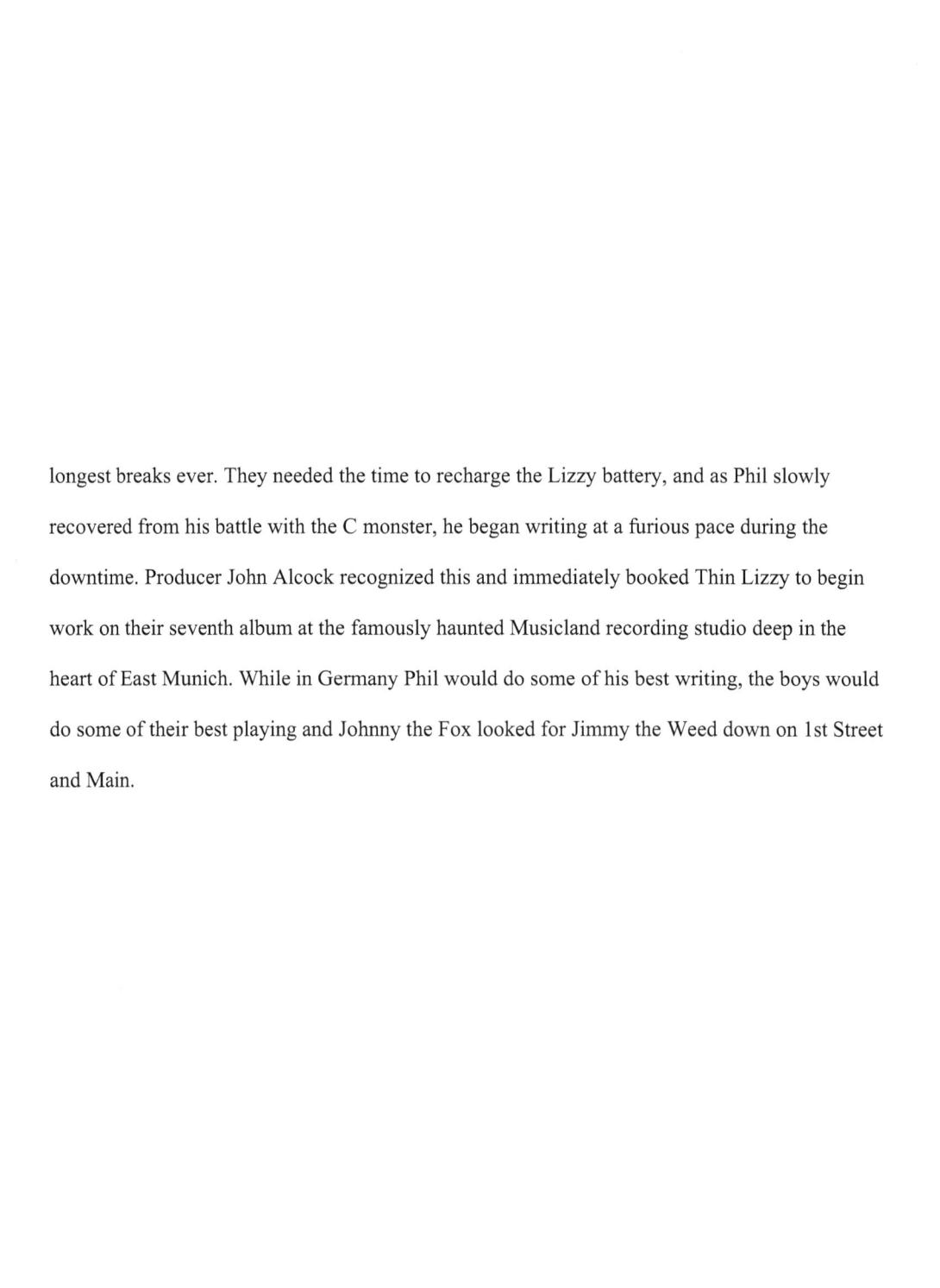

The Rockers

The noon's grey golden meshes make

All night a veil

The shorelamps in the sleeping lake

Laburnum tendrils trail

The sly reeds whisper to the night

A name-- her name-

And all my soul is a delight

A swoon of shame

James Joyce

While Phil recovered, he kept an acoustic guitar and notepad by his side at all times. Writing lyrics and working out chord arrangements for what would become Thin Lizzy's seventh album Johnny the Fox. Brian rested in Ireland while Scott and Robbo stayed at the flush Victorian home of their publicist, running through a number of ideas together trying to maintain the creative energy still left over from the Jailbreak album. During a visit by Sounds magazine's

John Ingham, Scott talked about the sudden success of Jailbreak, the unfortunate timing of the aborted American tour and the upcoming recording sessions scheduled in Munich. The reason for recording in Germany according to their producer Alcott was for tax purposes only. Which Scott thought was hilarious, because despite finally achieving mainstream recognition - Thin Lizzy wasn't exactly rolling in the dough. Distracted by the color television and Robbo's frequent applauding, Scott chugged his beer and shared his thoughts to Ingham while watching Arthur Ashe dominate Wimbledon. Scott shared his experience on recording Jailbreak and how it differed from their previous albums:

The previous ones we did in a sort of clinical way. I'd have my two songs and Phil would have his five, Brian Robertson would have his two, and that was it. 'Let's work on Phil's,' or 'Let's work on Brian's,' but on Jailbreak we all dived in on everybody else's songs, putting parts we had for our own songs into other people's. John Alcock (the producer) was a great guy to work with, he's got a lot of good ideas, he's easy to work with, a good man for sussing out when you're in the mood and when you're not in the mood. He's by far the best guy we've worked with. I really respect him. He'll be with us in Germany, seeing all the frauleins over there. It's a good place, Munich. We try to walk into the studio with a lot of ideas already fixed. Rehearse for a couple of week's first, talk all the ideas out, play them out. Just work it to death and then walk into the studio with a really good idea of what's going to happen. But we'll still change things or write a song in itself – I like that – walking into the studio and writing a brand new song nobody's heard before and seeing how it comes out. That's what happened with 'Emerald'. It's a lot of fun. Jailbreak is a kind of a concept but not a concept, if you know what I mean. It just happened. [14]

Three weeks after this interview Scott, Robbo, Brian, and Phil were on their way to Munich to begin recording the follow up to their gold selling Jailbreak. With a top shelf album under their wings, Lizzy was booked into the A-list recording Studio Musicland, located in the basement of the Arabella building complex and Hotel in Eastern Munich. Owned and operated by electronic and disco music pioneer Giorgio Moroder, a legendary producer and composer with three Academy Awards to his credit. Moroder recalls:

I had actually set up the Studio for myself. Hardly had I finished, someone by the record company called and said: Marc Bolan of T. Rex urgently needs a Studio for two months. I've rented it because it was good money, and when Bolan was done, I could work one or two weeks. Then phoned Ian Stewart, who at that time was the pianist for the Rolling Stones…After the stones came Queen then Elton John came, so it went off…I knew many studios throughout Europe, and almost all were uncomfortable, square. I wanted a studio where the musicians feel comfortable. There was a couch, a table where you could eat. And because a hotel was up, the musicians with the elevator could go home. [15]

Before closing in the 90's, Musicland was considered one of the greatest studios in all of Germany. With an iconic four decade run that included a list of who's who of the rock and pop world. Everyone from David Bowie, Freddie Mercury and Queen, Led Zeppelin, the Rolling Stones, Elton John and more have once poured out pieces of their souls in the microphones of the Munich music machine. Donna Summer's worldwide hit and disco genre kick starter "I love to love you, baby" was recorded at Musicland along with Led Zeppelin's Physical Graffiti, Bowie's "Golden Years", Black and Blue by the Rolling Stones, and Iron Maiden's classic metal album Seventh son of a seventh son, all of which comprise a tiny portion of the astonishing works recorded at Musicland. But perhaps the most important happening to ever take place was the famous 'Idiot Sessions' with David Bowie and Iggy Pop. These sessions in August of 1976 were produced by master soundman and experimental engineer Phil Palmer resulted in Iggy Pop's classic album The Idiot that included the original version of the future Bowie classic "China Girl". During the recording of this song and the mixing of The Idiot album, Palmer was experimenting with guitar overdub sounds and effects while using Thin Lizzy's equipment. The boys recorded during the day and left their gear in the studio at night without ever knowing that David Bowie and Iggy Pop were secretly siphoning some of their musical mojo!

By the mid-seventies, Munich had become the music capitol of Germany and with the sought after Helios mixing console, Musicland was ground zero. By the middle of August Thin Lizzy were recording songs for Johnny the Fox there but soon grew disappointed at Reinhold Mack, the studio's engineer. Brian's drums weren't crisp enough, Phil's compositions weren't completed and arguments over which musical direction to take became daily arguments and the only remedy to these clashes was more booze. After a couple of non-eventful weeks in Germany, Lizzy headed back to Alcock's Ramport studios in Battersea where they recorded their previous work Jailbreak. An album that brought them fame and fortune, and elevated Lizzy from opening act to headliners poised for superstardom. However, by the time they were recording Johnny the Fox, the buzz created from their commercial breakthrough had vanished. With the added pressure of having blown a chance to extend their run in America by Phil's illness, Lizzy faced the daunting task of recording an album with the thought of fame slipping through their fingers.

Hoping to find some of that same magic they discovered while recording Jailbreak the boys dove headfirst once again to fifteen-hour sessions under the watchful eye of John Alcock. The magic was still there and for the second time in 1976 they delivered the goods. Johnny the Fox, their 7th album was released in October in the UK on Vertigo and in November in the USA on Mercury. It peaked at #11 in the UK and #52 in America and became their second Gold album of 1976. The only drawback of the album was that it didn't contain another smash hit as the lead single "Don't believe a word" failed to set American audiences on fire despite reaching #12 in the UK and #2 in Ireland.

Despite not having a hit single the album itself is a real jewel and clearly outclasses everything save for bits and parts of Jailbreak, Lizzy had done prior to that point. It's full of musical virtuosity and is the apex of the twin guitar style done to harmonizing perfection. Brian's epic drum work branches into so many trailblazing paths that it's hard to even put into perspective. Phil's writing is top notch and reflective of his brush with the grim reaper. He pours out a wide range of emotions vocally and lyrically has mastered his gift for poetic storytelling accompanied by scene setting musical melodies. The album has so many moods and vibes that it seems to cast a spell forcing you to listen, an astonishing work of art that draws you in and challenges you to unravel the mystery of Johnny the Fox.

The epic album cover designed once again by Lizzy artistic director Jim Fitzpatrick, details a fox overlooking a hanging moon surrounded by Celtic totems. When Fitzpatrick began to design the cover, the album was still untitled and Fitzgerald's main center motif was blank. As his deadline approached he begged Phil for some ideas, Lynott famously replied, "Ah, call it Johnny the Fox, that'll do," and Fitzpatrick added the fox and the title giving birth to another half-baked concept album. Both Johnny and the fox are featured players in the album, and one gets the feeling that the fox is the Jekyll to Johnny's Hyde. This Johnny character had already appeared in the song

"Showdown" and in the summer smash, "The Boys" but on the first song on the Johnny the Fox album he struts his rocking ways as a doomed junkie headed to an early grave.

It's a powerful way to kick off the album and scorches the mind with a grimy and realistic portrayal of where the darker side of drug addiction can lead. Phil's lyrics are five stars, and his vocals are emotional, gut wrenching and delivered with an unforgettable amount of attitude. The music kicks off with a terrific riff, delayed guitar layers and crunching drums that roll and break beautifully throughout. Johnny's ill-fated story begins as Phil sings convincingly…

Somewhere on the waterfront Johnny's hiding with a gun

Swears he'll kill any man that tells his story

He's not sorry for what he's done

He broke into a drugstore

To cure his daily need

He didn't mean to shoot the guard

But he was blinded by the greed

Oh Johnny

You see that nun, she's his sister

She doesn't know that he's gone bad

When they told it to his father

It drove the old man mad

Just as his mother warned him

From her dying bed

It's alright to lose your heart

But never lose your head

Oh Johnny

Now the cops have got him surrounded

And he doesn't stand a hope

He wonders how he could be in so much trouble

Over just a little dope

Five to one he gets away

That's the odds I'm going to give

Five to four they blast him away

Three to one he's going to live

Oh Johnny

Back in the alley where he was slain

I thought I heard something move

Beside the trash can lay a heart and chain

The picture had been removed

Just another juiced up junkie

Looking for a bed

It's alright to lose your heart

But never lose your head

A spectacular duel guitar clash ends the song and leaves your heart pounding. This vibe is perfectly matched by the next song "Rocky" a tune with pounding drum work full of thudding cymbals. The song is about a young guitar wizard that pulls all the chicks. Phil was in fact writing about Robbo, and he lived up to the billing with ferocious riffs all over the track. Unfortunately, when released as a single it didn't take off. Robbo scored a co-writing credit on the album's third song "Borderline", a ballad sung beautifully by Phil. Written by Robbo and edited by Phil, it's a tune inspired by a girl breaking Robbo's heart. The music is mellow and the acoustics sweet, Scott delivers a fantastic solo and overall it is an excellently arranged track.

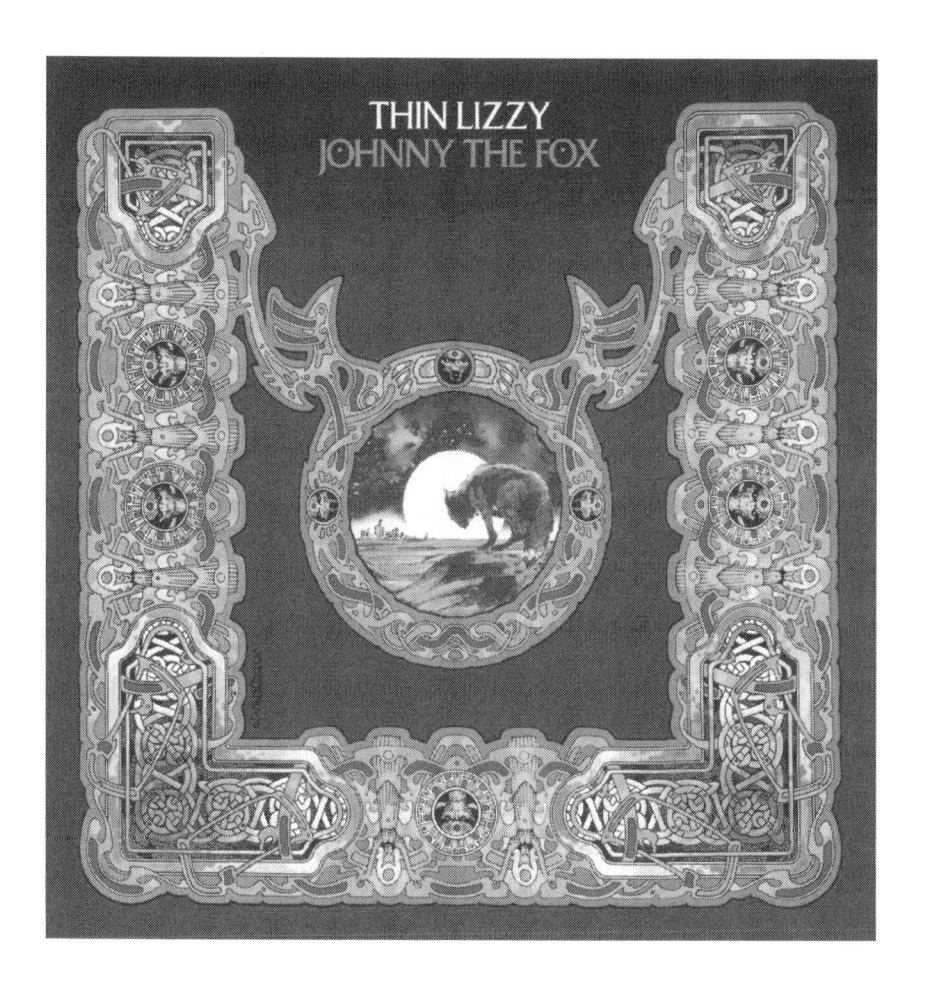

The fourth song on Johnny the Fox "Don't believe a Word" is an instantly recognizable Lizzy classic and rightfully so. A commercially friendly tune with great lyrics it was a hit in the UK but somehow failed to stir up any excitement in America, going nowhere upon its release overseas. Phil delivers with smooth vocals and Don Juan songwriting…

Don't believe me if I tell you not a word of this is true

Don't believe me if I tell you, especially if I tell you I'm in love with you

Don't believe me if I tell you that I wrote this song for you

There just might be some other silly pretty girl I'm singin' to

"Don't believe" was also the beginning of the end for Robbo's tenure as full time Lizzy guitarist. He clashed excessively with Phil over the sound style that the song should be played in, Phil wanted an original slow 12-bar blues take and when Robbo called it "Shite" the two got into a huge argument and shoving match resulting in Phil disappearing for a few days to cool off. While Phil was away Brian played peacemaker and began to work with Robbo on constructing a musical compromise. Picking up the tempo with a shuffle rhythm layered by Robbo's riffs, Phil was pleased how the beat turned out a few days later when he resurfaced at the studio. However, upon the track's release Robbo was pissed that neither he nor Brian received any credit on the song. While it is true that Phil wrote the lyrics, there should have been two extra credits for Robbo and Brian's work on "Don't believe a Word". Phil had a chance to explain his lyrics in an article found in the April 9th, 1977 edition of New Musical Express:

Don't believe a word is a reflection of Rock's bedroom battle of the sexes. You go through the whole process of chattin' up the chicks...and playing the game...giving them the old line...and I reckon most fellas will say just about anything to get a girl into bed...So that's how I came to write 'Don't Believe A Word'. It's just to say, if you believe every line a fella hands you, you'll only get hurt. [16]

The album's fifth track "Fools Gold" was inspired by the hordes of Irishmen that left for America during the Irish Potato Famine of 1845–1852. It's a beautiful song full of brilliant moments including Phil's smashing vocal performance, a simple yet lush chorus, a duel guitar solo, and backing riffs all painting the picture to one of Phil's greatest lyrical achievements. Phil's warning about chasing the illusionary effect of gold was written during a deep introspective period during his sickness and recuperation. It also is the first introduction of the mysterious fox character. The fox ends up stealing the show, the song, and of course triumphantly saves the girl. The track opens with a spoken word piece that's complimented by an angelic vocal chorus. Phil tells three amazing stories in one of the highlights of his poetic career…

In the year of the famine when starvation and black death raged across the land

There were many driven by their hunger to set sail for the Americas

In search of a new life and a new hope

Oh but there were some that couldn't cope

And they spent their life in search of Fools gold

The old prospector he makes it to the four lane highway

His old compadre, he lays dead in the sand

With outstretched hands he cries, "Are you going my way?"

The people passing by didn't seem to understand

The fox continues his scene stealing ways on the albums sixth track "Johnny the fox meets Jimmy the weed". A song that is as funky as anything you'd come to expect from James Brown or Isaac Hayes. It has great Shaft style shakers and guitar wah's, cool lyrics and grimy Donald Goines style storytelling far ahead of anything the funk genre was producing in America during its time. Proving that by this time Lizzy had become such accomplished musicians that if they wanted to make a funk album they could have done it easily and with stunning results. "Johnny the fox meets Jimmy the weed" has proven to be one of Thin Lizzy's most influential songs. Mostly for Brian's innovative drum work, which has been sampled in dozens of hip-hop songs including De la Soul's "Keeping the faith" and DJ Shadow's "Megamix" amongst others. It is also officially considered by the Crate Kings to be one of the greatest breaks of all time and is featured on the Ultimate Breaks and Beats series, an anthology essential to any serious DJ. Brian's drum work even branched out into influencing techno territory when electronica trailblazers The Prodigy sampled "Johnny the fox meets Jimmy the weed" for their worldwide smash hit "Breathe" in 1995. Phil's cool lyrics make you feel like a hustlin' ass pimp looking out for shady fools in the backstreets of Harlem…

Johnny the Fox he called to Jimmy the Weed

He said "Hey man, I know your name"

I seen you cruising with the low riders

Hanging out down on First street and Main

Tuned into and listen to the voodoo Rhythm Devils

Around the Bay

They've got some crazy DJs

Send you right out to heaven

Jimmy the Weed for greed was taken aback

Johnny the Fox you old sly cat

Cleverly the Fox concealed his stash

Crisp dollar bills leave no tracks

In the back of a black Cadillac

The voodoo music travels

Down Skid Row only black men can go

The shady deal unravels

Johnny the Fox, hot to hustle

Jimmy the Weed won't use no muscle

That cat's so sly, slick and subtle

Johnny the Fox breaks out the bottle

Tuned into and listening to

The voodoo music travels

The beating drum for the lonely one

The seventh track on the album "Old Flame" is a great romantic ballad named after a reference to an old Irish expression that was used to describe lost female friends of the past. An excellent love song everyone can connect with.

The eighth track of the album is perhaps its best one and essentially ends the album because tracks #9 "Sweet Marie" and #10 "Boogie woogie dance" are throwaways. Producer Alcock claimed that after completing "Massacre", which Phil wrote in the studio, they were spent and Lizzy's mojo exhausted. Used up in one hell of a year. The vibe and mix of the song is top shelf and once again Brian's drumming stands out as the groove plods along under an amazing array of heavy riffs and a dynamite solo by Robbo. Phil's lyrics are spectacular, and heart aching when delivered…

There goes the Bandolero Through the hole in the wall

He's a coward but he doesn't care though in fact he don't care at all

The General commanding, defending what we fear

The troops, they are depending on reinforcements from the rear

If God is in Heaven How can this happen here?

In God's name they use weapons

For the massacre

There's a point below zero

Where the sun can see the land

Six hundred unknown heroes lie dead beneath the sand

"Massacre" was inspired by a confrontation Phil had with a Protestant clergyman while recovering in the hospital. In 1977, Phil, profoundly told Melody Maker that:

Massacre came about when I was in hospital. I was amazed how much violence there is on the telly. How much death and destruction. I was really taken back…Y'know one day, you look at the television and it's no longer that friendly object that entertains you. It starts intrudin' in your home, tellin you that that somebody chopped somebody to bits. I was lyin' in hospital having to watch it because there was fuck all else to do…It just seemed to go on and on, and at that very time a knock came on the door. In came a Reverend. I was born a Catholic and I'm not very devout, but once a Catholic always a Catholic. It always has you. It's a real frightnin' religion, y'know. They always have you thinkin' in the back of your head that maybe it's true. They claim you when you're young. But he came in and asked if I would like visitors - you know, the way they do the rounds in hospital, just in case you want any, spiritual counseling. He knew, like, that I wasn't into it. When he left I thought 'Nice man, doin' his gig', but then the two things connected and I really thought and began to say: 'God are you doin'?' I thought I'd take on God. Why not? So I'm saying: 'If God is in the heavens how could this occur, because in his name there are religious wars and they use weapons to cause massacres. [17]

Most rock historians think that Johnny the Fox failed to live up to the impressive commercial standards set by Jailbreak. An unfair labeling because as the case in all Lizzy albums they seem to exist in their world separated both artistically and spiritually from one other. Johnny the Fox is a jewel of an album that showcases Lizzy on the verge of hitting their musical peak. It's full of tunes both catchy and dangerous, ballads that verge on cheese but never go overboard and lyrics that if presented in a poetry book only, would have won the hearts and minds of the sophisticated literary world. Phil's Johnny can be easily seen in Hollywood passed out next to a bottle in a ritzy hotel room with some naked chick he won't ever see again. Johnny the Fox also featured a young unknown drummer named Phil Collins on a couple of tracks. Brian saw that Phil had great potential and invited him to the studio for some added experimentations. However, as time passed on Brian couldn't remember what songs Collins worked on. Phil Collins of course went on to fame and success working with Genesis and literally created one of the best songs of the 80's "I can feel it coming in the air tonight".

Johnny the Fox is musically diverse and full of attitude, rocking hard in some places while getting funky and soulful in others. Back on tour in October to promote the album in the UK, Lizzy was delighted that Johnny the Fox stormed its way victoriously onto the charts reaching #11 and bringing them their second gold album of 1976. The tour was a major success and gave them their biggest crowds yet. An unknown American band Clover, which was led by Huey Lewis, supported them. Another future superstar of the 80's, Huey was a young and struggling musician that Thin Lizzy helped out by giving a break. Huey would later go on to speak very highly of Phil and admitted to the Dallas Observer on July 20, 2012, "Philip Lynott taught me most of what I know. He taught me more than anybody else. He was my main mentor. That band was so amazing live, such a great hard rock band." [18] The UK tour was so successful that extra dates were added at the Hammersmith Odeon in November and Thin Lizzy even upstaged Rod Stewart on his own BBC variety television program.

Things were going great and the buzz created by Johnny the Fox was beginning to spread over in America. But as was the usual case with Thin Lizzy bad luck was waiting around the corner. On the eve of their departure for the American leg of the tour, Robbo was involved in a fight that would have unfortunate consequences for everyone involved. At 4 a.m. when he should have been either sleeping or packing Robbo received a nasty hand injury from a glass bottle while defending his friend and Lizzy contributor Frankie Miller during a brawl at the Speakeasy Club in London. Frankie Miller's face was almost shredded by a jagged beer bottle by rival guitarist Gordon Hunte. Robbo blocked the serrated bottle to protect Frankie's face and as a result the saw-like bottle ripped apart Robbo's hand, slashing an artery and damaging nerves. The wound bleed profusely and Robbo was rushed to the hospital, leaving him sidelined from any guitar playing for months. This badly timed injury was severe not only to Robbo's hand but to the rest of the Thin Lizzy members, who were all devastated upon finding out that because of Robbo's injury their major tour of America scheduled to begin at the Palace Theatre in New York City had been canceled. It was a staggering blow and halted the momentum of the Johnny the Fox album in its tracks. Scott told the BBC how Robbo's injury deflated the band:

We were on such a great run at the point. Mentally, physically, playing wise and I mean everything. We just knew that that tour was going be the tour that was gonna break us. And it's kinda hard to get the stars all lined up again to get you know that kind of feeling again. This one hurt real bad. [19]

Because they weren't able to promote the album with a tour in America it bombed in the States, failing to chart higher than #50 on Billboard. It was a huge setback and Phil's vision and hopes of continuing the success of Jailbreak in America would forever go unfulfilled. As a result of

Robbo's ill-timed injury the band turned to the comforts of booze, women, and copious amounts of marijuana. Phil promptly fired Robbo while a new drug named cocaine began to circulate within the halls of Thin Lizzy's encampment. During the final weeks of 1976, Phil and Scott were invited to the listening party for Queen's upcoming album A Day at the Races at Advision Studios. Phil and Freddie Mercury were instantly enamored with each other, and they began discussing the possibility of touring together with Queen in the future. As 1977 loomed the boys now without Robbo, had no idea what would be in store for them other than partying, rocking, boozing, chasing chicks and stuffing large amounts of cocaine up their noses - habits that cemented Thin Lizzy's image as a band with a bad reputation.

A Bad Reputation

There is a pit of shame, and in it lies a wretched man

Eaten by teeth of flame, in a burning winding-sheet he lie

And his grave has got no name

And there, till Christ call forth the dead, in silence let him lie

No need to waste the foolish tear, or heave the windy sigh

The man had killed the thing he loved

And so he had to die

And all men kill the thing they love

By all let this be heard

Some do it with a bitter look

Some with a flattering word

The coward does it with a kiss

The brave man with a sword

Oscar Wilde

By the middle of January, Thin Lizzy was back in America looking to reclaim some of the momentum they had lost after Phil's illness and Robbo's injury. With Robbo now sidelined with a destroyed hand, Lizzy stalwart Gary Moore replaced him during one of the most important tours of their career. It was destined to happen as Gary Moore recalled, "I think Phil was having trouble with Robbo for some time and he wanted me back in the band. When they were originally going to be going to the States Phil mentioned that we ought to have a chat when they got back. Then the Speakeasy incident arose and fate intervened, before I knew what was going on I was heading for the States on one of the biggest Lizzy tours ever, from a profile view at the very least."

With the Lizzy addition of Moore now matched with Queen's Brian May, the tour became a guitar lover's wet dream that would have been a magical sight for those lucky enough to have seen it. Freddy Mercury and Brian May were already fans of Thin Lizzy's early albums, especially the Bell contributed masterpiece Vagabonds and hit it off so well with Phil and Scott at the A Day at the Races preview and after-party it was immediately decided that Thin Lizzy would be Queen's opener during an upcoming winter tour of America, a slot that many bands of the time were dying for.

Queen gave Lizzy a huge break and introduced them to their biggest crowds so far and by Phil watching Freddie Mercury completely own his audience every night, it gave him ideas galore and an added boost of confidence. Lizzy's first show and opening set during the 'Queen Lizzy' tour was in front of 11,000 fans at Detroit's Cobo Arena, and they dove into it hungry, raw and ready to rock. Harry Doherty wrote about the now famous tour in Melody Maker in an essay aptly titled "The Year Queen Lizzy Shook America". Setting the stage about what was considered "The greatest tour in the world at the moment" Doherty writes:

The winter of 1977 was fierce on the East Coast of the USA, a thick layer of snow engulfing the territory between Boston and New York. This freezing environment was to be the killing ground for two of Britain's biggest rock bands. Queen were at the height of their creative powers, having captured the world with 'Bohemian Rhapsody' and A Night at the Opera, now consolidating their position with 'Someone to Love' and A Day at the Races. Thin Lizzy, too, were no slouches. 'The Boys Are Back in Town' and its parent album Jailbreak had finally given them chart status, and this was sitting well with an awesome live reputation. 'Don't Believe a Word' and 'Johnny the Fox' emphasized their intention to stay around a while. Live and Dangerous, which would turn out to be rock's definitive live album, was just round the corner…Lizzy are the support band on the tour, playing an hour-long set compared to Queen's one hour and 45 minutes. As support, they are under the usual restraints, no thunderflashes, no wandering into restricted areas of the stage marked only for Queen use. One night Gary Moore broke out of Lizzyland and into Queendom, delivering a blistering solo in the process that brought the crowd to its feet. He was warned not to do that again. There's no animosity between the bands, though. Lizzy see it as a bit of a learning curve. "There were about a dozen bands that wanted to do this tour with us," said Roger Taylor. "We thought that Lizzy suited our audience better than any of the others, and they're probably better that any of those bands anyway.

Doherty continues after greeting the bands in New York City:

I joined the Queen/Lizzy tour in New York and was taking in Madison Square Gardens, Nassau Coliseum, Syracuse Civic Center and, finally, the Boston Garden. As an avid Lizzy AND Queen fan, this was my dream tour, the sort of thing you jot down during boring college lessons under "Great Tours I Would Like to See". Never having seen Gary Moore during his earlier (brief) stint with Lizzy, I was particularly keen to see how he would fit into the setup. He was a hired gun this time, taking over from the popular Robbo, and now having to play Robbo's set pieces and solos. How would this sit with Moore? I shouldn't have worried. Moore's input reflected his own effervescent style, adding a powerful injection of axe style. He was also an inspiration to Gorham, who seemed content to play second fiddle to Robertson but now brought out of his shell. So what, we all wonder, does the future hold for Lizzy and Moore? The band seem, wisely, to have left their options open. [20]

Scott recalls the tour and how the sudden replacement of Robbo with Gary Moore breathed fresh air back into the group:

I thought it was going to be a real tough one. It took Brian and me two years to get to where we were as dual lead guitarists, and when we decided that Brian was out, I was a little bit more freaked than anybody else. But after just eleven days rehearsal with Gary, it clicked. We worked on the harmonies a lot and I'm taking more leads than before. It's hard to say why there's more harmony work with Gary. Brian was more into playing lead guitar, and after a while he lost some interest in the harmony things so we were starting to do less and less of it. But Gary likes it as much as I do, so that reintroduced the harmony guitar work into Thin Lizzy. Playing with Gary is the happiest I've been for a long, long time. It's like breathing fresh air again. I guess it was kinda getting stale for a while. I know that on the last English tour, I was getting pretty depressed with a lot of those gigs. I would go back to the dressing room and I wouldn't talk to anybody, and just go back to the hotel and lock myself in there. There was really a lot of heavy raving going on. People were losing control of themselves, and it wasn't making for good music. It seemed sometimes that just a lifetime of noise was coming out, although we did have our nights when we came off and felt great. Brian was drinking pretty heavily, and I was going a bit crazy, too, and Phil, of course, still had hepatitis and he would get depressed. So this whole thing is just one big blast of fresh air, where everybody has perked themselves out of the staleness. We've got a new vibe in the band now. When we walk on stage, we have a great time again. It's like a whole brand new thing, with 100 percent more music coming out of it now. [21]

Doherty continues:

It was Thin Lizzy's first tour of the American East Coast. Through their series of misfortunes - first Lynott's hepatitis and then Robertson's hand injury - they never reached New York and the surrounding states until last week. You could smell the disappointment in the dressing-room afterwards when they felt that they didn't do their music justice at their first-ever gig there. The band never quite clicked. They had, said Lynott, treated Madison Square Garden as just another gig. Scott Gorham sat in a corner totally depressed by the whole affair, annoyed that this prestigious venue had not seen Lizzy at their best. The disappointment was such that Lizzy wouldn't go back on to do their encore; they didn't feel they deserved it. Syracuse, in New York State, was another gig where Lizzy did not work as they should. Here Moore was having difficulty with his guitar, damaged earlier in the day, and never settled down, while Scott Gorham was just a little too laid-back for comfort. Lizzy went down well at both places, but for this band, it's the sub-standard gig that breeds the excellent one, and it was significant that on the nights following the Garden and Syracuse, Lizzy went on to play concerts full of controlled aggression and anger.

After their disappointment at the Garden, Lizzy reclaimed their form with a smashing performance at Nassau Coliseum, in front of 20,000 devoted Queen fans. Lizzy were forced to work hard to win the support of the audience, a challenge they thrived on. They simply battered the crowd into submission with a hard-hitting set, marked by the performance of Gary Moore, who left members of the audience stunned by some of the solos he was producing. Brian Downey's drum solo during "Sha La La" sent the crowd into frenzy and they wasted no time in showing their appreciation for Downey's energetic wrestling bout with his kit. The gig ended with "Baby drives me Crazy", which evoked the right "baby, baby, baby" response from the audience, instead of the embarrassing silence of the previous night at Madison Square Garden. The atmosphere in the dressing room was much more positive than the previous night, with Lynott triumphantly announcing, "We showed 'em. We made an impression tonight all right. Follow that." Lizzy managed to surpass the success scored at Nassau three nights, later, in Boston, a city they've never played before and which, apart from "The Boys Are Back in Town" which everybody knows, is unfamiliar with their music. This time, Lizzy took only five minutes, and, by the end of "Massacre", the second number in the set, they sensed that it was their gig. Lynott, for one, was showing more aggression and portrayed his tough man persona to the hilt. It was an excellent tour for Lizzy and they made Queen work harder than they have ever had to before. To most American rock critics the underdogs had upstaged their masters.

Scott remembered how the tough Thin Lizzy homophobes handled Queen's massive gay following during a show at Winterland in the gayest of all American cities San Francisco:

So, we were up first and I'm blasting away and rushing about the left hand side of the stage, thinking I'll go and mess with the audience on the right. The spotlight is chasing me, and I get over there and look up and there's like five hundred of the gayest guys I've ever seen, man. They were wearing sequin hot pants, satin jump suits, huge floppy hats with waving ostrich feathers, and they're jumping off their seats throwing feather boas in the air. As soon as I arrived at their side, they all started lunging at me shouting, "Yeah! Shake it boy! [22]

Despite Scott and the rest of Lizzy's early unease, Freddie Mercury won them over easily with his charisma, leadership, overall talent and general awesomeness. They learned a lot more than just music by hanging out with Queen.

Guitar legend and Queen's musical director Brian May had nothing but love for Thin Lizzy. He said, "I have great memories of working with Phil and the Lizzies in the rock and roll decade of the seventies…to me Phil was a kind of Jimi Hendrix of the bass guitar. It wasn't necessarily through virtuosity, but through presence and command. Phil wrote and played from an honest heart, directly to the people."

After the successful American tour, Thin Lizzy returned to England and looked forward to a possible re-teaming with Queen for a summer tour of the UK but unfortunately this never happened. Another setback occurred when Gary Moore promptly quit the group again to further his solo career, leaving Scott to pull double duty on the guitar. In May, they got the good news that legendary producer Tony Visconti had agreed to produce their next album at his home studio in Toronto. Robbo was invited back to the group as a session player, Phil was leery of hiring him on a full-time basis and in fact Robbo is only credited on three songs on the album. For Lizzy the chance to work with Tony Visconti was a confirmation of hitting the big time. They had earned the respect of the fans, media and most importantly their peers. Looking back on Visconti's profound influence on music production over the last forty years makes the feat even more impressive.

In 1967, Brooklyn native Visconti journeyed to England seeking studio production gigs and soon found himself working under the tutelage of British soundman and Beatles collaborator Denny Cordell. Three years later he was one of David Bowie's early supporters and ended up playing on and producing Bowie classics such as Ziggy Stardust, Low, Heroes, Lodger, The Man Who Sold the World, and the album that helped launch Bowie's career Space Oddity. He was also responsible for Joe Cocker's spectacular debut With a little help from my Friends, and Marc Bolan's T. Rex albums. By the time it came to start recording Bad Reputation Visconti had settled into the married life and was a new father. He had been warned about Thin Lizzy's wild reputation but was shocked when it lived up to the hype. He describes his first meeting with Phil and Scott:

Being a father and studio owner brought a certain air of responsibility and sobriety. I didn't expect a stretch limo to pull up outside my modest home and two inebriated rock stars to get out, waving large opened cans of Foster's lager. The rock stars were Phil Lynott and Scott Gorham…Producing T. Rex and Bowie records hadn't prepared me for the way these lads lived and worked! You can't argue with a 6-foot-3 Irishman! [23]

A few days later Visconti met Brian and an angry Robbo at the studio as the band hunkered down to record their bleakest but best sounding album yet. Robbo wouldn't cheer up and felt that his reduced role was an insult. He later admitted that he was "a complete asshole" and should have been more mature about the second chance that he was given. He refused to hang out with the boys after the sessions and mostly sat alone in his hotel room until being called in to record at the studio. When given the chance he absolutely shredded on guitar but his ho-hum disenchanted attitude along with his drinking made the vibes a little too rocky for everyone involved. Visconti recalls:

Robertson looked every inch a rock lead guitarist and didn't walk anywhere without a bottle of Remy Martin in one hand. He was very, very angry, too. Phil Lynott took me aside and explained that they were having problems with him. I never knew what the problems were but Brian wasn't talking to the others and only managed to muster a curt "hello" to me…But Robertson never really climbed out of his blue funk. When it was time for his solo overdubs I asked him to play a bit for me to get a sound. Then we cut him loose. He would play brilliantly every time and if there was some suggestion I threw at him, he would oblige me and play it without resisting. But his bad mood prevailed even when we were all cheering in the control room after he played something brilliantly. Once we asked him to come in and hear his solo (a really great one), and he shouted "No!" and put his guitar down and walked out of the studio.

Bad Reputation definitely marks the turning point in the history of Thin Lizzy. It also turned out to be Robbo's final performance with the band, something he and the fans never seemed to get over. It also marks the beginning of Phil's spiraling descent into drug abuse as he struggled to cope with fame and rising over the immense bar he had raised for himself. Confronted with a change in his psyche, he lets it all hang out on some of the darkest, deepest and lyrical songwriting efforts he has ever produced. Vocally he was in top form and even Visconti was impressed that Phil did ALL of the vocals, including backing and chorus overdubs on the album, showing a tremendous amount of range. Thin Lizzy's third act was unfolding in Visconti's home studio in Toronto while Phil's song crafting abilities hit its stride. With Scott handling most of the guitar arrangements, including the duel sound he had helped to perfect with Robbo, aided by Visconti's genius for constructing sonic pallets and Brian's locked in, heart pounding, metal before it existed drumming, all signaled that an inspiring musical breakthrough was about to commence. The albums opening number "Soldier of Fortune" blossomed with gong echoes, slow haunting guitars, and the latest sophisticated synthesizer sounds. Visconti adds:

The keyboard chores were shared between Phil and Robertson. Phil loved to play the string parts. On "Soldiers Of Fortune" you can hear the strange synth parts and phased cymbals in the intro, plus a real gong played by Downey. Immediately you can tell that this is Irish rock music from the use of Celtic modal scales and subtle rhythms that remotely echo Irish folk dancing.

Phil tricks us into believing that an epic war song is about to take place, but instead forces us to listen a provocative anti-war song inspired by the soldiers returning home from Vietnam, soldiers now broken, mentally wrecked, dependent on pharmaceuticals and ignored and pissed on by their Government. A theme that unfortunately hasn't changed much in America, a nation that is still fighting bullshit wars in foreign lands, occupying more than 130 countries worldwide with military bases and drugging their disposable soldiers on more pills than Phil Lynott could have ever imagined. In fact the suicide rates amongst American soldiers are at an all-time high.

A short but mouth-watery solo by Scott during a lush tempo change, floating synths and a military drum beat by Brian all add an incredible amount of texture and depth to one of Thin Lizzy's finest musical moments. When the song kicks in again before Phil's closing chorus, Brian's drums are neck snapping and absorbent while Scott masters the duel harmonic guitar sound all on his own. It's a beautiful way to kick off an album and fades out with flair to the sound of gongs crashing, perhaps signaling that Johnny was finally dead. From a Circus magazine article written on September 29, 1977:

Lyrically Lynott has sharpened his sensibilities, spinning diverse tales this time as varied as "Soldiers of Fortune" and the American depression. Lynott dropped Johnny. While looking for new antiheroes to immortalize, Lynott heard about James Callender, an Englishman who last year was thrown out of the British Army in Ireland and died while fighting as a mercenary in Angola. The displaced soldier's tale became the inspiration for the opening track. [24]

The album's title track "Bad Reputation" is an adrenalin-pumping arena sized rocker that represents that vintage Thin Lizzy sound. With heavy riffs, rolling bass, crushing drums mixed and panned to perfection and a blistering solo by Scott, this song would go on to be another set list staple and cherished Lizzy anthem. Three decades later it was featured in the popular video game Guitar Hero II, appeared on the soundtrack of the award winning 2001 documentary film Dogtown and Z-Boys and has been covered by hip-hop-metal pioneers 24-7 Spyz and the Grammy winning group The Foo Fighters. Although Scott was at his best on this song he can barely remember doing it, "I recollect making the album much more vividly than the actual song. Weird shit was going on in those days, we were just a threesome, Brian Robertson was recovering from an accident…When we ended the tour we decided to record 'Bad Reputation' with only me, Phil and Brian, hence the 3 faces on the album cover." In the August 27, 1977 edition of Sounds Phil explained the idea behind the song:

Yeah, well I just liked the idea of 'Bad Reputation' Lizzy were definitely getting a bad reputation around. The interviews before we went away were like Brian Robertson was drunk and getting into fights. Scott was always talking about his hippy days when he was a drug addict. My interviews always seemed to be about my sex life and Brian Downey just didn't speak at all. There seems to be very little talking about music. [25]

It's also a clever warning to get your shit together before it's too late…

You got a bad reputation

That's the word out on the town

It gives a certain fascination

But it can only bring you down

You better turn yourself around

Turn yourself around

Turn it upside down

Turn yourself around

You had bad breaks well that's tough luck

You play too hard too much rough stuff

You're too sly so cold

That bad reputation has made you old

The third song on the album "Opium Trail" is pure genius, daring, unequaled and an eerily prophetic ode about drug addiction that foreshadowed the eventual vice that would be Phil's downfall. It was silent cry for help that was too cool and provocative to be taken seriously. It also features some astounding guitar shredding from Robbo in what would be his swan song in playing for Thin Lizzy. It's an epic display of record producing by Visconti, full of special effects, mixing experiments and rock opera worthy moments. Phil's lyrics are among his best and the storytelling verses told in the poetic styling of the Romantic era are delivered with a haunting, soulful croon bringing the doomed storybook to life. Phil paints an impressive lyrical portrait...

I took a line that leads you to the opium trail

Oriental eyes reveal the lies, deceit, betrayal

On this journey behold the one who travels far

You called him fool but now you are

The wizard wanders through the world we made from dreams

The splashing whirlpool drowns the frightened screams

Exotic dancers, flashing lenses, this mysterious space

The fanfare advances, the warlord falls from grace

Powerful lyrics that would begin to haunt the band more and more as 1977 rolled on. Tour manager Frank Murray remembers:

The problem was that we'd all been hitting it a bit heavy - smoke, drink, coke, and so on. But then Philip started taking tranquilizers; he'd do all this coke to keep him awake until five in the morning, and then take a load of sleeping pills to get himself to sleep. Then there'd be someone knocking on his door a few hours later trying to get him on the bus to the next town. Consequently, he'd usually be in a really foul mood, and he'd be looking for a fight. [26]

Before Phil slipped into full-blown heroin addiction, it seems that he wrote, "Opium Trail" as a warning to himself. It failed. Phil was already on a heavy dose of cocaine, booze, sleeping pills and tranquilizers and was knocking on the door to the home of every musician's poisoned golden apple. Visconti recalls the early warning signs that would ultimately end the doomed rock star:

Of all the people I worked with, Phil was the most genuine rocker...Drugs were a staple for Lizzy. I believe they really killed Phil in the end. I can't help but think that Phil was sending out a cry for help with this song. I once questioned his ability to play stoned. He replied that he'd been smoking dope for so long he could play extremely well stoned. According to Phil, it was the others in the group who shouldn't get high, not having the experience he had!

Following the epic "Opium Trail" is a lazy Californian sounding song called "Southbound" that once again showcased Phil's continual fascination with American themes. The song's subject matter focused on the hordes of Americans on the move West after the Great Depression and was inspired by The Grapes of Wrath, a book written by Nobel Prize winning American author John Steinbeck in 1939. Phil somehow found the time to read and devour the book before recording sessions for the album began. Phil was a huge admirer of Steinbeck and "Southbound" is a homage to the man who wrote what many consider to be the Great American Novel. The song starts with excellent riffs by Scott and a cranky bassline accompanied by some excellent jazzy relaxed shuffle drums by Brian. The hook is sing-along friendly and the guitar solo marvelous. Visconti brilliantly layers some smooth harmonica melodies during the solo that fit perfectly. The fifth song on Bad Reputation doesn't sound like a Lizzy at all. In fact if you heard it being cranked out on Top 40 radio you would nod your head, snap your fingers, boogie with a smile and then be utterly shocked when the DJ announced that it was a song by Thin Lizzy! We're talking of course about "Dancing in The Moonlight (It's Caught Me in Its Spotlight)" one of Thin Lizzy's most signature songs and as a band of serious musicians and songwriter's one of their crowning achievements.

Thin Lizzy were miles apart when compared to other bands of their era and their ability to produce hard rocking arena burners alongside intricately catchy R&B numbers truly justifies why they have been able to maintain such a lasting appeal decades after the sands had run out of Phil Lynott's hourglass. Who would have thought that a fucking sax could help make a Thin Lizzy masterpiece? Although the song confused American radio stations who didn't know where to play it and to what audience, it was a smash hit in the UK and shot to #14 on the Singles Chart when released in September. The bass groove by Phil is top notch funky and Scott's solo short but inspired and Brian's breakdowns before the chorus are seductive. Phil channels Sam Cooke and sings with a ton of soul...

When I passed you in the doorway

Well, you took me with a glance

I should have took that last bus home

But I asked you for a dance

Now we go steady to the pictures

I always get chocolate stains on my pants

And my father he's going crazy

He says I'm living in a trance

But I'm dancing in the moonlight

It's caught me in its spotlight

Dancing in the moonlight

On this long hot summer night

It's three o'clock in the morning

And I'm on the streets again

I disobeyed another warning

I should have been in by ten

Now I won't get out 'til Sunday

I'll have to say I stayed with friends

But it's a habit worth forming

If it means to justify the end

And I'm walking home

The last bus is long gone

But I'm dancing in the moonlight

Tracks #6 and #7 on the Bad Reputation album fail to match the impressive first half and fall into a lull where they don't add much to the incredible thus far listening experience. "Killer without a Cause" is a smashing metal cut better suited for live performances. It's Robbo's second contribution on the album and he plays furiously on a voice box like the one made famous by Peter Frampton. But overall the riffs are just average and Phil's lyrics are pretty subdued. Following "Killer" is the boring ballad "Downtown Sundown" where John Helliwell plays clarinet and Phil sings cheesy vocals about love and god. Track #8 "That woman's gonna break your Heart" is a galloping Springsteen inspired number that Scott manages to get a decent riff on, but loses steam midway with a corny attempt at slapback overdubs. Robbo makes his last appearance as a member of Thin Lizzy here, but it's sad to say that the duel harmonic two-headed monster had seen better days. Bad Reputation culminates with the spectacular spiritual epic "Dear Lord" a track that shows Phil at his best.

Powerfully written, heartbreakingly soulful and sincere in its delivery, "Dear Lord" is a masterpiece that broke new ground in rock production. Layered with sound effects galore, sweeping guitar melodies and floating cymbals and high hats, and the added bonus of Visconti's then wife Marry Hopkin's angelic backing vocals it's a beloved Lizzy classic and timeless testament to Lizzy's vast amount of musical talent.

Bad Reputation was released in September and quickly soared to #4 on the UK album charts and went Gold in just four weeks. It was another smashing success in the UK and a huge leap forward in production and song writing but as usual failed to spark the excitement and interest in the United States that Jailbreak had managed to do. The album cover was void of a Jim Fitzpatrick art piece and as the front cover suggests most of the tracks were made with three-quarters of the band. Robbo's auspicious absence on the album cover proved ominous, as he would never appear again on a Thin Lizzy album. With another hit record and single to promote Thin Lizzy, including Robbo were back on the road and playing to sold out audiences in a fall European tour. They had never been bigger or more admired or influential. Accepted by critics, the media and the fans, Phil was finally a full-fledged rock star. Something he had always dreamed of being. Harry Doherty, the famed rock journalist that wrote for Melody Maker claimed:

When at their best Thin Lizzy was the best live rock n' roll band in the world. Nobody could touch them. They knew that Phil was a great front man. Scott knew that he looked good. Phil knew that Scott looked good. Robbo was so arrogant he thought everyone looked good and Downey was the muse who knew everything. [27]

They drove around in a limo that was typically Thin Lizzy with a wire hanger holding down the trunk to keep their squished up gear in. As their fame and fortune rose during the closing of 1977, so did Phil and Scott's reliance on drugs and alcohol. With bona fide rock star success came the demons that accompanied that journey and both Phil and Scott, although not seemingly too worried, jumped head first into crippling vices and self-destructive lifestyles. Stephen Thomas Erlewine of Allmusic reviews Thin Lizzy's classic eighth album:

If Thin Lizzy got a bit too grand and florid on Johnny the Fox, they quickly corrected themselves on its 1977 follow-up, Bad Reputation. Teaming up with legendary producer Tony Visconti, Thin Lizzy managed to pull off a nifty trick of sounding leaner and tougher than they did on Johnny, yet they also had a broader sonic palette…Of course, they were stripped down to a trio for most of this record: guitarist Brian Robertson (who'd injured his hand) had to sit out on most of the recording, but Scott Gorham's double duty makes his absence unnoticeable. Plus, this is pure visceral rock & roll, the hardest and heaviest that Thin Lizzy ever made, living up to the promise of the title track. And, as always, a lot of this has to do with Phil Lynott's writing, which is in top form whether he's romanticizing "Soldiers of Fortune" or heading down the "Opium Trail." It adds up to an album that rivals Jailbreak as their best studio album. [28]

As the sun set on 1977, Thin Lizzy closed out the year with a string of sold out shows at the Odeon and looked forward to once again working with Tony Visconti. Soon they would begin mixing what many consider the greatest "live" album of all time.

Living Dangerously

On Raglan Road of an autumn day I saw her first and knew

That her dark hair would weave a snare that I might one day rue

I saw the danger and I passed along the enchanted way

And I said let grief be a fallen leaf at the dawning of the day

On Grafton Street in November we tripped lightly along the ledge

Of a deep ravine where can be seen the worth of passion's play

The Queen of Hearts still making tarts and I not making hay

Oh I loved too much and by such by such is happiness thrown away

I gave her gifts of the mind I gave her the secret signs

That's known to the artists who have known

The true Gods of sound and stone

And words and tint without stint, I gave her poems to say

With her own name there and her own dark hair-like clouds over fields of May

On a quiet street where old ghosts meet

I see her walking now

Away from me so hurriedly my reason must allow

That I had loved not as I should a creature made of clay

When the angel woos the clay he'll lose his wings at the dawn of day

Patrick Kavanagh

1978 was a busy year for Thin Lizzy that started off with a popular European tour and a filmed performance at the Rainbow later released on video as Live and Dangerous. But Robbo's tenure wouldn't last long and by the end of July his official stint as the other half of the famous duel guitar sound ended in a bullring in Ibiza. Phil then tried to evolve Lizzy into a Frank Zappa styled jam band called the Greedy Bastards, a troupe that was designed in part to avoid paying the tools at the IRS. It was a move that didn't last long but created a lot of buzz among the punk crowd. The Greedies first show on July 29th, brought in Gary Moore, and Phil begged him every night to join Lizzy once again. Their first show got underway with an all-star lineup that featured Paul Cook and Steve Jones from the Sex Pistols, in a wild Lizzy/Pistols Mash up.

Phil was an early supporter of punk rock and his stature amongst the punks was one of high respect. Punk music dominated the scene in late 70's London, but since Phil and Thin Lizzy were the original punks, they got a pass and were respected greatly. Besides every punk rocker who picked up an instrument in 1978 already knew that Thin Lizzy's musical craftsmanship was amongst the most respected of the times. Thin Lizzy could fucking play and by the middle of

1978, this was a fact that nobody could ignore. Phil's Greedy Bastard experiment lasted only half a year and featured an all-star lineup that included Jimmy Bain, Chris Spedding, Bob Geldof, Johnny Fingers and Rat Scabies.

Phil was also doing more features and solo work that year. He jammed with Elvis Costello a few times, and sang backup vocals with fellow Irish rocker Bob Geldof on the Blaster and the Heatwaves EP Blue Wave. He produced a 7-inch single "Fight your heart out" for Brush Shiels that was only released in Ireland on Hawk records and has since become highly collectible. He produced and featured on the Johnny Thunders album So Alone, and even helped Gary Moore have a hit single with the beautiful ballad "Parisienne Walkways" penned by Phil. Phil's contribution on his old friend Gary Moore's first true solo album Back on the Streets would prove to be deal sweetener in persuading Moore back into Lizzy. But Phil's most fascinating contribution to the arts in 1978 was his involvement in Jeff Wayne's musical spectacular The War of the Worlds. Inspired by the H.G. Wells novel, Wayne adapted the book into a musical opera with lyrics written by Elton John lyricist Gary Osborne and featuring narration by Oscar winning actor Richard Burton with singers from the cast of Evita. Engineer Geoff Young, who used then state of the art synthesizers and 48 track-recording techniques that represented the first of its kind.

Phil was assigned the spoken word role of Parson Nathaniel. Despite having no acting experience Phil nailed his performance during "Sprit of Man" and even did a decent job hiding his Irish twang while speaking a London accent. The eleven-minute song features Broadway legend Julie Covington and when Phil sings alongside her he stands his ground. The song is dark and inspiring, contains a subtle Lizzy element and Phil was perfectly cast as the doubting savant.

Jeff Wayne's opus The War of the Worlds would spend 290 weeks on the UK album charts and reached the top 10 in 22 different countries. It is a classic album that has sold millions of copies around the world.

But Phil's most significant act of 1978 was his beaming rock god image of slumped knees wrapped in tight black spandex, while holding his bass like an M-16 rifle firing imaginary bullets into a glowing spotlight. This of course is the iconic picture that graces the cover of Thin Lizzy's ninth and most acclaimed album Live and Dangerous.

A double LP composed essentially of Lizzy's greatest hits that were recorded during the band's musical peak in 1977. Recorded during Thin Lizzy tours in support of the albums Johnny the Fox and Bad Reputation, the Live and Dangerous album was totally unplanned and a result of spur of the moment studio brilliance. It came about after Phil learned that working on a follow up to Bad Reputation with producer Tony Visconti would take at least a year because Tony's schedule had become so clogged up.

Phil was already pissed off at the massive success of Peter Frampton's live album that seemed to be mailed out to every home in the suburbs in America, and came up with an idea of Visconti producing a live album for them. To Phil this was an instant light bulb going off over your head moment. Lizzy's reputation was built off being a solid live band and with Visconti's studio wizardry the result might end up being the best chance at capturing a Lizzy live concert properly on record. Visconti was sold on the idea and managed to secure a few weeks at his Good Earth Studios in London to work on the project. He describes the making of one of rock's landmark albums:

Bad Reputation was a big hit. That meant Lizzy and I would get a second chance to create a great album. Unfortunately, they caught me between a Bowie album and at least three other projects I had committed myself to produce…Phil said that they had stacks of tapes from live gigs, so why didn't we spend two weeks going through the tapes and come up with a decent live album? That was the best we could do in two weeks. Hah! For the next eight weeks I was up to my eyeballs in Live and Dangerous! We listened and listened and listened -- to at least 30 hours of tape recorded during many gigs, from Toronto to Philadelphia to London! We definitely had something, but the task of choosing the right takes was awesome. When we did, Phil asked if he could touch up some vocals. No harm in that -- this is commonly done for live albums because of technical faults, like microphone wire buzz and other gremlins. The trick to getting a studio vocal to sound like a convincing live vocal is to sing the song in the same way. Otherwise the live voice will poke through if the new voice is not in sync. We spent a few days re-recording a few vocals. It went very well. Once we established a sound and a system to do this, Phil suggested that we might as well redo all the vocals. So we did. Then we noticed that Gorham and Robertson were not on mic for backing vocals half the time. If you listen closely you can hear Phil doubling the backing vocals at the same time he was singing lead! Then Phil realized that he'd missed a few notes on the bass when he was singing live. Could we replace some bass parts?

"Of course!" I said. We did. The bass was harder and more precise and so ALL the bass parts were replaced. In walked Scott Gorham and Brian Robertson. Since it was so easy to replace Phil's parts, could they redo theirs? "Of course!" But now it was obvious that this was not completely live anymore. The guitars, bass and vocals were replaced -- just Downey's drums and the audience reaction were left! Fortunately Downey liked his playing and we kept ALL the drums…Every track was performed before a live audience with the exception of "Southbound". There weren't any good takes of the song recorded in concert, so we used the recording made during the sound check onstage in Philadelphia and dubbed in the intro and outro audience reaction from that night's show. Because the original recordings lacked certain details I had to resort to some trickery when Phil asked for audience participation. For instance, on the breakdown of "Rosalie" Phil asks the audience to "put yer hands together" I boosted up the audience tracks and there was a wildly enthusiastic audience clapping like mad, but the band was far louder. I couldn't use those tracks because the band would've sounded too echoey, picked up by the high audience mics. So I made a 20-second loop of the audience clapping for an encore. I put the loop through electronic gates that were triggered by a note from a keyboard. The loop was silent until I played a note on the keyboard. So when I played quarter notes (crotchets) it sounded like the audience was clapping along. Remember, they'd been clapping along that night but the mics just didn't pick them up loud enough. Also, at the end of this track the tape ran out and I had to edit in the audience reaction from the end of another song. That's why it literally sounds like a burst of applause at the end. Despite the necessary trickery this album is very real. It represents electrifying moments before an audience and fabulous second chances to get it right in the studio. [29]

Visconti's recollection pertaining the mixing of Live and Dangerous and how many overdubs and what percentage used has been famously challenged by Robbo who claims that Visconti is full of shit. Robbo swears that he didn't overdub anything other than a few guitar licks. Robbo sets the record straight with Matt Blackett from Guitarplayer.com:

Matt: It's a persistent story in the music business that there's not much live playing on Lizzy's live record, and yet that's not your recollection.

Robbo: It's not my recollection, it's not Brian Downey's recollection, and it's not Scott Gorham's recollection. This is down to Mr. Visconti. Let me get this straight because this is really starting to piss me off.

Matt: I didn't mean it to be a hostile question.

Robbo: I'm not being hostile towards you at all. The only person I'm being hostile to is Tony Visconti, who I hold in great esteem. I just don't understand why he's come out and said these things. He has said, "It's 75 percent overdubs." What the fuck drugs is he on? I'd like some of them. Think about this for one second and then you can make your own mind up. We're playing live, the drums are all miked up, all the vocal mics are open. We are a very loud band, me being the loudest out of all of us. So how are you going to replace my guitar when it's so loud that it's going to bleed all over the bloody drum kit? You can't! It's perfectly impossible. There's no way, when Robbo's using two Marshall 100s cranked up to ten, that it isn't going to spill over to the drum tracks. This is why I don't understand this bollocks that's going on. Here's another point. When we were mixing Live and Dangerous, there was one take of "Still in Love with You" where my solo was just unbelievably brilliant. I'm not being a big head here, but when we heard that take I went, "That's the one." But Phil Lynott had left his phaser on and it was turned so fast that the bass was going "wow wow wow." So why didn't Tony Visconti just fix the bass track? Because he couldn't overdub the bass. You know why? Because the bass stacks were next to the drums and the bass was bleeding all over the drum mikes and everything! There's your answer right there. End of story, really. I'll go to court with the guy over it.

Matt: Did you do any overdubs?

Robbo: I think the only thing we overdubbed was a couple of little licks on Scott's guitar— because he played a lot quieter than I did— and a couple of backing vocals. I think Phil put one or two bass lines in and that was it. That is not 75 percent. Like I said, I don't know what drugs the man is on but he's talking absolute shit. I don't understand why a producer of the caliber that Tony Visconti obviously is would stick by this story. But hey, I love the guy—he's a great producer. I just think he needs to rethink his statements on this.[30]

Harry Doherty doesn't care how much overdubs were done on the album summing up the classic arena rocker perfectly, "There's a big dispute about what came from where. Who gives a shit? It sounds great you know and Visconti is the man who pulled that together." Visconti recalled the impact Live and Dangerous had on Bono and U2:

I have the distinction of Bono from U2 coming to me, when I worked with them later, saying to me - That was the most fantastic live album I've ever heard. It was a primer for us. That was our textbook for U2. We wouldn't be U2 unless we heard Live and Dangerous.

No matter how much overdubbing was done on the album, it sounds fucking great and for that we can once again thank Tony Visconti. Released in June, 1978 Live and Dangerous was an instant commercial and critical success that surprisingly rocketed to #2 and spent an amazing 62 straight weeks on the UK album charts. The only thing that kept Lizzy from claiming the vaunted number #1 position was the soundtrack for Grease. The album opens with the riot-inducing stomp of "Jailbreak" a track that features crushing guitar work and Phil's interaction with a dazzled crowd. The song magically fades into "Emerald" where Phil introduces it with one of the coolest delivered lines ever recorded live, "Has anyone got a little Irish in them? Are there any girls who'd like a little more Irish in them? This is Emerald." This song explodes from the speakers and is a stunning testament to the guitar virtuosity of both Scott and Robbo who provide fucking spectacular riffs and an unmatched duel that gains both of them instant guitar hero worship. The album continues to excel with "Southbound" a laid back track that Brian caps off with a gong. Brian doubles up on his great drum work with "Rosalie" and the band shifts into a mellow breakdown with a quick teaser "Cowgirl's Song". The crowd is alive and energized and as soon as Phil's funky bass kicks in for "Dancing in the Moonlight" it's evident that the first five songs on the album are scorching and have successfully placed the listener front row in a Thin Lizzy concert. The song features a lovely live sax solo from John Earle of the Graham Parker band, that's followed by a kick ass solo from Scott culminating in a funky Lizzy performance. The laid back groove doesn't last long and soon the hammering twin guitar brutality of "Massacre" transports the crowd to the wild frontier. The song rocks hard and the musicianship of all involved are superb.

The seventh track is the highlight of the album and hard to believe that it was actually recorded live. The version of "Still in love with You" on the Live and Dangerous is considered the ultimate version of the song. It's beautiful and Phil's vocals are delivered to heart aching perfection. It also contains Robbo's shining moment of glory for Thin Lizzy as he delivers two solos that have since become legendary. After the funk number "Johnny the Fox meets Jimmy the Weed" Lizzy finally gets to some balls-to-the-wall rock with the album's best moment "Cowboy Song". A blistering display of musical virtuosity that opens as a slow ballad then blazes into shuffling rock anthem before cooling down as Phil asks for a little audience participation. The crowd responds with claps and cheers after being told by Phil that, "It's OK amigos you can let yourself go." The song ends by brilliantly shifting into the bands most famous song "The Boys Are Back in Town" a tune that gets the party going and the butterflies swirling in your stomach.

The album continues to shine up until the second to last track, an original blues number "Baby Drives Me Crazy" that only appears on the Live and Dangerous album. A song mainly used to introduce the band to the crowd, this particular version features an outstanding harmonica solo by Huey Lewis. It also has great crowd participation and easily illustrates the connection Lizzy had with its audience. Naturally the "Rocker" which showcases more excellent crowd interplay with Phil, closes out the album with authority leaving the listener wanting more. Ironically that's what it has done for more than three decades now as the Live and Dangerous album signals the last time the fab four sound of the definitive Lizzy lineup would ever be heard in all of their glory.

The final hurrah of Lizzy's classic era was thankfully recorded, mixed, mastered and preserved for future generations. From 1978 on, none of the boys would ever be the same and Live and Dangerous remains their crowning achievement of the time they spent together making everlasting music. Robbo remained in Lizzy long enough to promote the album for a few months upon its initial release in the summer of 1978, but was soon permanently fired.

He formed a band with Jimmy Baines called Wild Horses that Phil (who always considered him part of the family) helped introduce on British television. Despite obtaining a cult following Wild Horses failed to sell any records and broke up after two albums. Robbo joined the legendary Motorhead, but failed to make the stint last and for the past few decades has shuffled around in various bands while composing solo albums and keeping the memories of his experience in Thin Lizzy alive with boisterous and captivating interviews. The guitar boy wonder from Scotland definitely deserves more props and when it was announced that Thin Lizzy had regrouped in 2011 with original members Scott and Brian, true Lizzy aficionados were left punched in the gut upon hearing that Robbo wouldn't be joining them.

Thin Lizzy had the hottest album of the summer but once again, despite smashing the charts in the UK, failed to make the same impression upon America. Live and Dangerous was Lizzy's first release under the iconic Warner Brothers label but failed to reach higher than #82 on the billboard charts despite garnering positive reviews. Trying to understand why Lizzy could never achieve the same commercially successful status in America as they did with Jailbreak has become one of rocks greatest conundrums and for good reason. It just doesn't make sense! A review from the New Musical Express on June 3, 1978:

Ah now, this - this is a little more like it! Not only is this the eagerly awaited Lizzy double live album, easily the best live rock album since the Feelgood's "Stupidity", but it almost single handedly vindicates that hoariest battering ram of current cliché razor jobs: the trouncing of the live double album package. Because "Live and Dangerous" is the goods - that thrilling aural documentary that not only captures all the muscle, dynamism, cut and thrust and gorgeous brainplate scouring of being right there on the spot, but also - indefinitely more exciting - one of those of so precious 'live' albums that captures rock action at its purest, most senses-pillaging transcendent ascendant…Live and Dangerous is in fact a near perfect statement of intent by what is right now the best hard rock band in the world. It's certainly the band's finest recording yet - mating most of their finest songs with that positively lethal style of firepower hyper-drive they've mastered from the years of amping it out and honing it all down to the needle point.30

Tim Jones laments about the Lizzy masterpiece in the 2005 book 1001 Albums you must hear before you Die:

As Israel pulled out of Lebanon in June 1978, Thin Lizzy pulled out the stops with one of music's greatest live albums. Its airbrushed quality caused critical murmurs; manager Chris O'Donnell claimed the recording was "75 per cent live," with overdubs correcting Phil Lynott's overdriven bass and backing vocals from guitarists Scott Gorham and Brian Robertson. Producer Tony Visconti, told BBC Radio 1, "We erased everything except the drums...even the audience was done again in a very devious way...'Southbound' was recorded at a sound check, and I added a tape loop of an audience." Fans were not bothered. The result is magical, and Vertigo's fears for a full-price double album were unfounded -- it shipped 600,000 in the UK. [31]

Live and Dangerous has steadily become Lizzy's most respectable and critically acclaimed album, astonishingly defying the odds to become one of the defining accomplishments in rock history. The BBC recently heralded it as the greatest live album of all time, a distinction agreed upon by the voters of the UK's popular classic digital rock station PlanetRock.com who overwhelmingly voted Live and Dangerous as the greatest live album ever. But when the British music magazine NME also listed Live and Dangerous at No. 1 in its "50 Greatest Live Albums of All Time" 2011 special, it justified all the hard work the pioneering band had dedicated their lives to. Thin Lizzy had created a powerful musical testament that has stood the test of time. The decade's long commercial and critical recognition for Live and Dangerous has truly elevated Thin Lizzy's status as one of the world's greatest rock bands.

The boys had a genuine hit with Live and Dangerous and took to America for a fall tour to promote the album with Gary Moore replacing Robbo on guitar and for the first time in over a decade without Brian Downey on Drums. The exhausted Downey was replaced by Mark Nauseef and stayed in Ireland to rest while sorting out family matters. From August to October Thin Lizzy rocked arenas up and down the United States and performed alongside notable acts such as Kansas, Journey, Blue Oyster Cult, AC/DC and Styx. They continued their partying alcoholic ways and were at this point full blown hotel trashing rock stars.

While in Memphis Phil and Scott made a few attempts at recording in one of the legendary studios that littered Beale Street but after hearing that Jerry Lee Lewis hated black men, Phil took the streets searching for the old rocker intent on kicking his ass. He instead ran his car into someone else's, resulting in a furious car chase up and down the Memphis streets, being pursued by a pistol waving Barry White clone. Phil and Scott managed to make it back to their hotel avoiding any serious injury. A few nights later they opened for Kansas in front of 11,000 fans in Oklahoma City where naturally "Cowboy Song" brought down the house. They continued west and rocked more than 17,000 heads at the Forum in Los Angeles before joining Foreigner and the Steve Miller band for the Louisville Summerjam II at the Kentucky fairgrounds where they played in front of 40,000 people. In Chicago, they supported AC/DC at the Aragon ballroom and filmed a live segment for the American late night rock television show Midnight Special. Their American tour wrapped up in October, and the boys were surprised to be given an impromptu chance at rocking Australia and New Zealand.

They jetted out of LAX and a few days later were rocking close to a hundred thousand people during a free concert at the Sydney Opera House. They pulled out all the stops in a legendary performance that was recorded live by Australia's channel 7-TV. Later rebroadcast on television and released on home video the iconic performance of Lizzy tearing up Australia is a must see spectacle. The cops even had to shut off the power after the rousing "Cowboy Song" started a mini-riot. Phil was at his best and most confident and oozes the same rock god quality he inherited from Freddie Mercury a year earlier.

Thin Lizzy returned to London and closed out the year with a football charity event at Wembley and some Greedy Bastard shows. Phil was in complete rock star mode as he judged the Miss World Contest won by Argentina's Silvana Suarez at the Royal Albert Hall. By the end of December, Brian Downey was back in the band as they rocked the Hammersmith Odeon and Phil was given the go ahead from Warner Brothers and Tony Visconti to begin work on the bands next project. And this time Phil got his wish by successfully convincing Gary Moore to join them for long enough to record an album. Moore agreed and a long held dream of both Phil and Brian's was about to come true - An official album recorded with Gary Moore! As 1979 approached the boys appeared unstoppable and with the heavy buzz that surrounded the arrival of Gary Moore into Thin Lizzy, hysteria from fans and the media was at an all-time high. But underneath the rock god façade was the quiet realization that both Scott and Phil were secretly becoming full blown heroin junkies.

Black Rose of Death

My Dark Rosaleen

Over hills and through dales

Have I roamed for your sake

All yesterday I sailed with sails

On river and on lake

The Erne, at its highest flood

I dashed across unseen

All day long in unrest

To and fro do I move

The very soul within my breast

Is wasted for your love!

Oh, I could kneel all night in prayer

To heal your many ills!

And one beamy smile for you

Would float like light between

My toils and me, my own, my true

My Dark Rosaleen!

James Clarence Mangan

As 1978 ended Thin Lizzy were back in the recording studio, and Phil was still experimenting with his jam band the Greedies. They rocked a Dublin ballroom on a typically wet Irish night when rising rock stars U2 had the dubious task of opening up for them. Bono recalls the experience saying, "One of the Greedy Bastards came off stage, walked straight through the door (of the dressing room), threw up and then walked straight back on stage. Phil was at the end of Thin Lizzy and about to slide down the hill into the abyss. It was a strange moment. We really didn't know how dark it could get for guys in a rock band." Bono and U2's success was in part paved by Phil Lynott and Thin Lizzy. Bono has nothing but respect and admiration for Phil admitting, "He was an amazing frontman. If lyrical and musical ability has to be matched with showmanship, attitude, style, if that's your version of rock 'n' roll, there's no way past Phil Lynott. He's at the top of the tree."[32] U2 were still a decade away from topping the charts while Phil, Scott, Gary and a well-rested Brian began recording their tenth album Black Rose: A Rock Legend.

Once again for tax purposes Lizzy left the UK to record half of the album at Pathe Marconi EMI in Paris but returned to finish it off at Tony Visconti's Good Earth Studios in London. In between recording sessions Lizzy took off with Nazareth for a quick tour of America, where they tried out live some of the new songs they were working on. But the onslaught of a crippling heroin addiction began to rear its ugly head for the first time during those initial months of 1979 as both Phil and Scott got caught knee deep in its wrath. While in Paris, Phil sickly collapsed and spent three days holed up in his hotel room recovering with the help of holistic tea. Scott remembers how Paris was the wrong place to be for him and Phil during those days:

We literally used to get the drug dealers pounding on the door trying to get in and we let them in. Before then it was kinda recreational now of all of a sudden it starts to get serious. You know the smack starts to come in and whoa! Hey wait we haven't tried this yet, let's try this! That's the period where the drugs started to creep in to the band. Paris was the spot where the heavy stuff started to roll in.

Alan Byrne writes in Thin Lizzy:

The sessions evolved in a cagey and down beat manner as it became apparent that they coincided with Philip Lynott's immersion in heroin addiction. Though the material on the album is readily accessible, the tone and mood of the compositions are quite startling, drunks, drug addicts, death, love, sex all rolled into a complete but unstable lineup. Yet few suspected it, in an almost boastful way it prophesied the downfall of Thin Lizzy. [32]

Due to the drugs and alcohol Phil's creative energy and literary spark was beginning to waiver, but he still had enough in him to deliver another classic album to Warner Brothers. Black Roses' leadoff single "Waiting for an Alibi" was released on March 3rd and peaked at #9 remaining in the top ten for eight straight weeks. It's a classic Lizzy song with excellent guitar melodies, a monster hook and fantastic lyrical storytelling. The chart-entering single provided the band a healthy dose of optimism as they were set to follow up the success of their previous smash album Live & Dangerous. Phil once again asked Jim Fitzpatrick to design the album cover and he did so brilliantly. Inspired by James Clarence Mangan's poem "My Dark Rosaleen" Fitzpatrick designed an epic stylized black rose that even ended up as a tattoo on Axl Rose's right shoulder. The legendary Gun n' Roses singer wanted to show it to his idol Phil but sadly never got the chance. Black Rose was released on April 13th, 1979 and quickly made all the right noises with the buying public as it peaked at #2 on the British album charts. It would be the commercial high point for both Lynott and Lizzy, becoming Thin Lizzy's most successful studio album and to this day remains one of their more enigmatic recordings. Especially since it turned out to be Gary Moore's only full-length contribution to the Lizzy catalog after previous stints in '74 and '77 that only resulted in brief studio outputs. His shredding on Black Rose is unforgettable and there's no doubt Moore was at his peak, re-energized the band and shook Scott out of his complacent slumber.

With Moore's unchecked musical blues pedigree soaring high it inspired Brian Downey to follow suit and he produced his best drum work to date. Black Rose is unquestionably the bands crowning musical achievement, a fucking monster of an album that reached new heights despite Phil's downward heroin spiral. More than thirty years later it remains Lizzy's musical plateau, providing a fork in the road of their legacy that they would never return to. Another strange quality to the album is the eerie and prophetic mood and tone that the rocker Phil created. His compositions have unfortunate Nostradamus like accuracies regarding not only himself, but to the wider world's self-imploding that only a true poet can foresee and describe.

Sadly to most Americans this album remains an overlooked gem that failed to impress the Billboard charts, barely cracking the top 100 upon its initial release in 1979. While "The Boys are Back in Town" was still being played on American radio they totally ignored Black Rose and its accompanying singles. It's a shame. Thin Lizzy was becoming the unsung heroes of rock and their latest album offered up another dose of beautiful melodies, expert musicianship, powerful lyrics and a dark post-punk world full of characters that you were better off meeting only in your headphones. In a sense, Black Rose is Thin Lizzy's last hurrah. Greg Prato of Allmusic writes:

Black Rose: A Rock Legend would prove to be Thin Lizzy's last true classic album (and last produced by Tony Visconti)…also turned out to be the band's most musically varied, accomplished, and successful studio album, reaching number two on the UK album chart upon release. Black Rose: A Rock Legend is one of the '70s lost rock classics. [33]

Black Rose was released to widespread critical acclaim and followed in the footsteps of Live and Dangerous matching its peak at #2 on the UK album chart while spawning three hit singles. The album explodes with the inspiring opening track "Do Anything you want to Do" that combines Brian's tribal African drum groove with impressive social commentary by Phil…

There are people that will investigate you

They'll insinuate, intimidate and complicate you

Don't ever wait or hesitate to state the fate that awaits those

Who try to shake or take you

Don't let them break you

You can do anything you want to do

It's not wrong what I sing it's true

You can do anything you want to do

Do what you want to

People that despise you will analyze then criticize you

They'll scandalize and tell lies until they realize

You are someone they should have apologized to

Don't let these people compromise you

Be wise too

You can do anything you want to do

It's not wrong what I sing it's true

You can do anything you want to do

The song fades out with great shuffle drums and Phil impersonating one of his heroes Elvis Presley saying, "The King is dead", reflecting on Elvis's recent death. Phil would later pen a whole song dedicated to the king of rock n' roll on his solo album. The video shot for the single "Do anything you Want To" was the band's first short film that wasn't the typical miming along to the song in a supposed live setting while standing in a film studio sound stage. It shows Lizzy playfully banging on large conga drums intercut with shots of overlord police figures and pompous judges. At one point Phil stresses his views from a jail cell and as a professor in a classroom. It's a great video that would have had a bigger impact if only MTV had been around in 1979. From the April 14th, 1979 issue of Sounds magazine Phil explains the songs meaning:

The opening lines are very anti-critics…it's about when people can't understand you and then proceed to blindly criticize you for not doing what they think you ought to be doing. At least the kids who catch this tour will be given a chance to make their own minds up. And on the other level it's about what you can achieve. People say success is a God-given talent, that only the chosen few are allowed through the door but if you really want it you can achieve success. If you work at it, if you apply the effort you can achieve your aims. [34]

The second track on the album "Toughest Street in Town" is a heavy dose of urban reality, and full of great chord progressions and a wickedly fast solo by Moore that Visconti mixes perfectly with echoes and phasers. Brian's drums rip and roar all over the mix and Phil sings like he's preaching from a back alley. It's interesting to note that Phil's original set of lyrics were rejected by the record company for being a little too real…

Like a rat in the back, the junkie opens his packet of smack,

On his arm there's a track, that he can't take back,

On the corner is a man w/a tattoo on his right arm

It's there as a constant reminder of grievous bodily harm

Phil was forced into a quick rewrite before the final mastering that still told the junkies plight of daily street violence to bone chilling perfection…

Outside the window the neon flashes

In the morning light

Down on the sidewalk there's a woman with a problem

But she don't know how to fight

She's destitute and broken down

She softly whispers is there no one around

And no one hears the sound

The drums that blast through the third song on the Black Rose album are justifiable proof that Brian Downey is hands down top ten one of the greatest drummers that ever lived.

The drums on "S & M" cascade from jazz to metal and are once again mixed and panned to perfection by Tony Visconti. By this point in the album it's becoming abundantly clear that Brian's drumming was going to be stealing the show. The bassline delivered by Phil is grimy and epic and musically speaking the guitar work and underlying melodies all funk off Brian's inventive driving drums and hi hats. Scott delivers one of his finest solos ever. It's clear that Moore's influence and tenacity had a positive effect on the laid back Californian. Phil's lyrics were decades ahead of their time and can be considered Fifty Shades of Grey meets Thin Lizzy. "Waiting for an Alibi" begins with a catchy bassline that is one of Phil's best. It's dirty and funky and when silhouetted by a plush harmony works well. This was the big hit on the album and is commercially solid with a tight, catchy hook and dueling guitars that are vintage Lizzy. Despite the mainstream sound the lyrics are super cool as Phil expertly details the life of a gambling mobster. It's the archetypal Lizzy track that showcases the Lizzy sound at its finest, however by it failing to chart in America it inadvertently took all the steam out of the boys. The first side of Black Rose ends with the touching ballad "Sarah" a song inspired by the birth of Phil's newborn daughter. It was a dubious time to be a new father, due to the unfortunate timing of Phil's heroin addiction meshing with his drive to be a family man.

He named his daughter after his grandmother and in fact is the second Thin Lizzy song to be titled "Sarah" after his ode to his grandmother on the Shades of a Blue Orphanage album. Gary Moore surprisingly played all of the acoustic guitar parts and melodies. Scott didn't appear on the song but showed up in the promotional video, another great one that shows Phil all dressed up like a lounge crooner singing to a string of different young girls in a lounge. Huey Lewis didn't appear in the video but provided the harmonica sounds that complement the ballad nicely. The single peaked as high as #24 on the British charts and at #5 in Germany despite never being performed live by Thin Lizzy. In an interview in Manchester on November 16, 1979 Phil told Piccadilly Radio:

The media, they're always looking to define you in one short paragraph or in one quick sentence and the work they always pick on is the macho thing. To do a song such as 'Sarah' which is about my daughter is as lovey-dovey as you can get and what am I supposed to say? That I don't love my daughter? Music is an art form and it should surely reflect what goes on in your life.

You have a child, everybody has a child and it's a big occasion in your life. For me, I had to write a song. [35]

The second half of the album opens up with Phil's mournful cry for help "Got to give it Up" a deep song where Phil confronts his demons bravely head on. It's a stunning display of bravado, lyricism and profound risk taking realness that has stood the test of time as a dire warning about the dangers of drugs and alcohol. A song that has scared many into recovery, unfortunately Phil had to die so that others could live. Phil's vocal performance is amongst his best despite Visconti's recollections that many times during recording he had to prop up a drugged out Phil and that his drawl was influenced by his nasal passages being clogged up with cocaine. Although Visconti was disturbed and worried about Phil's increasing drug habit the results that ooze throughout the Black Rose album were spectacular, albeit doomed. Phil's ode to drug abuse takes on a new meaning when considering that as of 2015 drug abuse has hit an all-time high in America and the UK…

Tell my mama and tell my pa

That their fine young son didn't get far

He made it to the end of a bottle

Sitting in a sleazy bar

He tried hard but his spirit broke

He tried until he nearly choked

In the end he lost his bottle

Drinking alcohol

Got to give it up

I got to give it up that stuff

Tell my brother, I tried to write and

Put pen to paper but I was frightened

I couldn't seem to get the words out right

Right, quite right

Tell my sister, I'm sinking slow

Now and then I powder my nose

In the end I lost my bottle

It smashed in a Kasbah

Got to give it up

I've been messing with the heavy stuff

For a time I couldn't get enough

But I'm waking up and it's wearing off

Junk don't get you far

Tell my mama I'm coming home

In my youth I'm getting old

And I think it's lost control

Mama, I'm coming home

Got to give it up that stuff

Got to give it up

You know what I am talking about

Phil talked about his issues with drug abuse, specifically heroin in a no nonsense interview with Good Morning Britain in 1984 - A mere year and half before his untimely death. Phil doesn't sugar coat it and the five-minute interview is real as it gets. Phil's willingness to talk about such a risqué topic to some moronic talking head makes for great viewing and thankfully a clip of the conversation has been preserved on YouTube. Phil was truly a once in a lifetime sort of artist that even while educating the masses, was still unable to break free from the vice grips of an image that he wholeheartedly created for himself. The bloated rocker profoundly explained the role heroin played in his life:

The frightening thing about heroin is…again without trying to glamorize the drug at all, is that it's a very enjoyable drug to take. It cuts off reality. If you got a lot of problems and you just wanna (waves his arm insinuating to let go)…so it's very easy and it would be so easy for me to just jump up on television and say hey this is the pits don't do it. But the thing that's never put across on television very well is how enjoyable it can be. But in that and after the initial phase then you become dependent on the drug. Now I never got to the stage where I became so addicted where me body craved physically for it but mentally that battle will continue for the rest of my life. [36]

Following the ballsy "Got to give it Up" is the weakest track on the album "Get out of Here" a fast boot stomping cut co-written by future part-time Lizzy member Midge Ure. The only thing worth mentioning about the song is Gary Moore's ravishing solo. Moore's reverberating fuzz fades into the next to last song on the album "With Love" an up-tempo ballad with bluesy lyrics. The song features great acoustic work and a fabulous solo from Scott while Gary provided the melodic harmonies and tasty outro. "With Love" is one of Phil's greatest love songs…

It's a tedious existence laying your love on the line

Resistance is useless she can leave at any time

I must confess that in my quest I felt depressed and restless

But this Casanova's roving days are over more or less

With love she broke my heart and made me sad

You foolish boy you lost what you had

The closing and title track of the Black Rose album is perhaps Thin Lizzy's greatest musical accomplishment. "Roisin Dubh (Black Rose) A Rock Legend" is a seven-minute epic about the Irish folk hero Cuchulain. But Phil doesn't stop there and manages to mix in and pay homage to a list of his literary and artistic Irish heroes including Van Morrison, Shaw, Byron, Joyce, Wilde, Yeats and Synge. It's not only a fitting end to a spectacular album, but marks the end of the golden era of Thin Lizzy. It's one of Phil's and the bands everlasting masterpieces, full of A-list drumming, bass work and complex chord changes and solos that showcased and proved beyond a shadow of a doubt what Thin Lizzy were all about. The song seamlessly blends through a progression of Irish melodies and songs that included "Shenandoah", "Danny Boy", and "Go Lassie Go". Gary Moore is at his absolute best here and even manages to get the sound of bagpipes mimicked to perfection equipped with only with only Les Paul's and Marshall Amplifiers. Gary patiently taught Scott the harmonies and with the help of super producer Visconti the results were jaw dropping rock god virtuosity light years ahead of its time. Phil explained his magnum opus to Sounds magazine in 1979:

It's based on legends, how legends and myths survive. Y'know Black Rose, Roi'sin Dubh, is the old name for Ireland. Initially you think I'm just talking about the past then I come up with fairly modern Irish lilts...Shenandoah' is an Irish-American song. 'Go Lassie Go' is Scottish. See at the time I conceived it Robbo was in the group and that was him, 'Danny Boy' is Irish, Downey and meself.

I brought it to the band about two years ago and they said it was too silly, but then Gary came back into the band and we worked on it together…At the end of the recorded version there's spoken lines like 'Oscar he's so wild' being Oscar Wilde, 'Brendan where have you been?' Brendan Behan, 'the joy that Joyce brought to me', 'Georgie he knows best'. I was trying to get 'nobody shouts like a Liam Brady' with 'it's a long way to Tipparary' but I couldn't get it in. Thinking back on it, it's saying there's so many things you can be proud of if you're Irish, cos there's so much bad press for Ireland.

"Black Rose" is certainly years ahead of its time. It is an unabashed tribute to Irish Celts, heroes past and present. This fabulous suite with its Celtic pride predates Riverdance by more than ten years. It would prove to be the final studio magic contributed by Visconti, who refused to work with Thin Lizzy again until Phil kicked his drug habit. Phil never did and Visconti's contribution to Thin Lizzy's production legacy sadly ended with Black Rose. Visconti recalls his decision to quit working with Thin Lizzy:

Black Rose was the beginning of the end. Things were going really, really well but there was a certain point in the album where Phil thought he could relax a little bit. He was drinking a lot. He would chop out copious lines of cocaine. There was three days were Phil was stuck in his hotel room and it was obvious this wasn't the flu or some sort of head cold. This was serious and I knew then that I couldn't work with him anymore. It was too hurtful for me. I mean I would feel that I can't watch this guy kill himself. He was killing himself. [37]

Phil's epic ode to Ireland…

Tell me the legends of long ago

When the kings and queens would dance in the realm of the Black Rose

Play me the melodies I want to know

So I can teach my children, oh

Pray tell me the story of young Chuculain

How his eyes were dark his expression sullen

And how he'd fight and always won

And how they cried when he was fallen

Oh tell me the story of the Queen of this land

And how her sons died at her own hand

And how fools obey commands

With Black Rose riding high on the charts the boys did a series of sold out shows amidst a UK support tour. This tour was cut short however due to the unrelenting presence of the police drugs squad. Knowing that Lizzy's bad reputation was now verifiable the pigs went undercover and disguised themselves as fans amongst the crowd. Lizzy's roadies were onto the jive and some quick thinking, drug dumping and lucky escaping saved Phil and Scott during shows in Sheffield and Bridlington. Needing an escape from the heat Thin Lizzy retreated to the Bahamas for two weeks where Phil worked on his solo album and the rest of the gang including Huey Lewis lounged by the pool sipping rum and smoking joints of killer island ganja.

A few months later Thin Lizzy were back in America touring in support of Black Rose but the stateside bad luck continued as history repeated itself. This time it wasn't Robbo who got the axe but instead Gary Moore laid the axe down. Disgusted by Phil and Scott's heroin problems, lackadaisical playing and overall lax attitude Gary Moore left Lizzy for good. Disappearing mid-tour during a show in Reno, Nevada and leaving Lizzy as a disenchanted three-piece for a couple of weeks until bringing in Midge Ure to unceremoniously replace Moore. The press had a field day in covering the latest Thin Lizzy fiasco, a band now gaining press not for their playing, but their out of control rocker ways. Gary explained the aborted American tour ordeal in an interview with the Record Mirror:

I felt that there was too much raving and not enough good playing, which got embarrassing when we got up on stage. I mean we were playing to some of the biggest audiences with Journey, they let us use their lights, PA, and effects. We just hadn't had enough rehearsals put in, and our record company Warners didn't even seem to know that we were in town. The tour itself wasn't handled all that well either. [38]

Thin Lizzy returned to England and did a few more shows before taking replacement guitarist Dave Fleet of Manfred Mann to Japan for a series of sold out and widely influential shows in Tokyo.

Lizzy flew back to England where everyone except Phil took a break. Phil returned to Good Earth to finish his first solo album, a project that he had been working on for at least eighteen months. He found the time to sing alongside Lesley Duncan and other notable British singers like Kate Bush and Pete Townsend in a corny single for charity "Sing children Sing". Phil made up for it with a new single from his alter-ego Lizzy/Sex Pistols combo band the Greedies. Releasing the Christmas mash up single "Merry Jingle" in time for the holidays and setting off a stream of punk appreciation and bad reviews.

But "Merry Jingle" looked upon from the 21st century is one of the coolest Christmas tunes ever made. Seeing members of the Sex Pistols alongside Phil, Scott and Brian rock a yuletide track live on the Top of the Pops is a magical punk rock moment. The only thing missing is watching Santa get the shit kicked out of him backstage. Phil Lynott and the Sex Pistols successfully closed out the 70's together on the Kenny Everett 1979 New Year's finale show and unknowingly ushered in a new decade that would soon kill the legend of Thin Lizzy.

Solo in Chinatown

Versing, like an exile, makes

A virtuoso of the heart

Interpreting the old mistakes

And discords in a work of Art

Thomas Kinsella

A new decade emerged and to the fans in the UK and greater Europe Thin Lizzy appeared to be at the top of their game. After a decade of relentless touring where they achieved both commercial and critical success Thin Lizzy had managed to write the blueprint for the working class rock band. Coming off back-to-back albums that reached enviable chart positions both at #2 Thin Lizzy showed no signs of slowing down. But beneath the Johnny cool fascia a new ugly truth was beginning to emerge. The heroin monster was slowly taking over both Scott and Phil's world and despite blowing up in the UK, the failure of matching the success of Jailbreak in America emotionally tore them apart. They couldn't understand why their post Jailbreak albums and singles failed to have an impact on the American public. Most of it was of course due to the incompetence of their record label but to the drugged out Phil and Scott it might as well been some satanic conspiracy. They filled the void of this loss by consuming alcohol and heroin, going overboard towards full-blown addiction. All the while preparing for the release of his solo album and getting married.

Phil Lynott's marriage to the daughter of famous British television game show host and comedian Leslie Crowther marked his acceptance into British high society. Crowther humorously told Phil after being asked for the hand of his daughter in marriage, "Well, you've had the rest of her so you might as well have her hand too!" a funny anecdote Phil retold numerous times during interviews. Before the wedding of course was the bachelor party, or as it's known in England, a stag party, and Phil's was legendary. Held at the Clarendon hotel in the Hammersmith and attended by an all-star of lineup of legendary rockers that included Billy Idol, Lemmy from Motorhead, Simon Kirke, Midge Ure, Jimmy Bain, the Dire Straits and everyone involved in Thin Lizzy amongst others. By the time the three strippers had arrived, everyone was already so smashed that it was hard to know who was still awake. Robbo recalls the evening with great memories, "His stag night was great, in fact we all ended up having a jam. There were lots of musicians there, and everyone was playing, singing, just having a good time basically. I remember Ozzy Osbourne getting up to sing a few numbers but God knows exactly who played with whom." A month later Robbo, Brian, Scott and the rest of the Lizzy brand from managers to the roadies all showed up dressed in suits to witness Phil's marriage to Caroline Crowther. Scott was Phil's best man and made the women swoon, especially journalist Paula Yates who marveled at how his new haircut showed off Scott's handsomely chiseled face to perfection.

The wedding was held during freezing weather at the picturesque St. Elizabeth of Portugal Catholic church in Richmond. It was a grand affair and a lovely moment for both Phil and Caroline's families. The newlyweds quickly jetted off to Brazil for their honeymoon and then returned a few weeks later to buy a new home in the ancient fishing village of Howth, a quiet setting on Dublin's Northern Coast. He then bought his mother Philomena a stunning home in Sutton that had a lovely view of the sea. Dubbed the White Horses estate it has since become a pilgrimage to the truest of Lizzy fans and admirers. While back in Ireland Phil rejoined the boys and began an Irish tour. Thin Lizzy added former Pink Floyd guitarist Snowy White as Phil replaced the more keyboard inclined Ure in hopes of matching Snowy's bluesy psychedelic riffs alongside Scott. Snowy had played opposite David Gilmore on the iconic Pink Floyd tours for The Wall and Animals and the announcement of him joining Thin Lizzy caused shockwaves and ripples of excitement amongst the English music community.

In April of 1980, Snowy joined Phil and the rest of Thin Lizzy at Good Earth studios in London to begin work on the bands eleventh album Chinatown. But Phil was also working on his solo album during the same sessions and with the extra pressure of being newly married and a heroin junkie the abuse began to take its toll, both physically and mentally. Scott was a wreck also and Snowy's assimilation into the band during the simultaneous productions of Chinatown and Phil's Solo in Soho while being handled by greenhorn producer Kit Woolven made the situation even more strained. Woolven was Visconti's apprentice and the unsung hero during the recording of Lizzy's previous three albums, but with Visconti refusing to work anymore with Phil until he cleaned up his act it left the young and impressionable Woolven to cave in to anything Phil wanted to do in the studio.

Most of the times the studio resembled a party full of onlookers, admirers, wannabees and groupies in scenes reminiscent of the last days of Jimi Hendrix. The Legendary Grammy winning Detroit bassist Jerome Rimson was present during these sessions and even played bass on one of the songs on Phil's solo album becoming the only other person besides Phil to play bass on a Lynott album. Rimson describes the wild sessions and Phil's gradual downfall:

I watched him record most of the Chinatown and Solo in Soho albums standing at a microphone and making up the words as he went along, and while he was singing there was a full blown party going on in the control room. Just think of it fifteen or twenty people in the control room raging while he's in the vocal booth trying to rescue these albums.

Snowy remembers how surprising and frustrating it was to see the accomplished poet reduced to freestyling lyrics while smashed during recording sessions:

A lot of the Chinatown album was made up in the studio, especially Phil's lyrics. He used to leave his lyrics until the very last minute then light up a spliff and head for the vocal booth and sing off the top of his head. Because he was such a perfectionist he was always changing things and thus it was very time consuming, delaying the album release even more.

The titles of both albums Chinatown and Solo in Soho were inspired by the neighborhood that Good Earth Studios resided in. Soho is the iconic arts district in the city of Westminster and is part of the famous West End of London. Long established as an entertainment utopia, for much of the 20th century and during Phil's stay, Soho had a bad reputation full of sex shops, streetwalkers, punks and junkies. It was also near London's Chinatown and could have easily provided the dragon chasing components Phil and Scott desperately needed. Smack, jamming and fried rice were the essential ingredients during these hectic recording sessions. To make matters worse Lizzy was back on the touring treadmill in May to break Snowy in for the live shows all the while failing to live up to their standards in the studio. Snowy wasn't the only addition to the Lizzy line up as Phil started to slowly introduce a keyboard element into Lizzy's hard rock sound.

Always a great recognizer of talent Phil was impressed by the keyboard virtuosity of seventeen-year-old Darren Wharton and gave him a shot by allowing him to work on some songs during recording sessions. When Wharton performed live with Lizzy during those initial gigs while still recording Chinatown and feeling out Snowy, it was a little awkward to witness coming from a fans perspective. The tour was a letdown and it wouldn't be until July that Lizzy actually had a single to promote with the release of the album's title cut "Chinatown". The single featured another series of excellent promotional clips and a main video that would have been another perfect match for MTV. Lizzy's music videos were certainly ahead of their time and if they had been made around five or six years later, then it's quite reasonable that Phil would have been either the first or second black man seen on MTV following or possibly preceding Michael Jackson. One could imagine the impact on America Thin Lizzy could have had if they had managed that feat!

The video's director David Mallet had done all of Lizzy's previous videos and especially loved the sleazy Chinatown red light district imagery and overall grimy vibe they created at the trusty Molinear Studios. Phil had put on a few pounds, and neither he nor Scott bothered to shave and can be seen sweating like fuck after spending nearly ten hours filming on a sound stage underneath a bunch of hot ass lights. Still the video rocked even though poor Snowy comes across as absolutely wooden.

Mallet remembers:

We got the atmosphere just right for it and it totally suited the song. Phil was always the gentleman in the group as were the others of course. There was always something about Phil that made you take notice. Often after the shoots, which might last anything up to ten or twelve hours, we'd head back to his place and stay up all night chatting. He was a very humorous guy who was hip without trying to be in the slightest. He was never the outrageous rocker at all which a lot of people tend to believe. In fact quite the opposite, the image in the papers is far from the Philip who worked with him still remember.

"Chinatown" peaked at a measly #25 and sank into oblivion nine weeks later, failing to secure another top twenty hit for Thin Lizzy. The magic was wearing out and it was foolish to follow up Black Rose with such a relaxed album. It was a costly stylistic oversight made all the worse by the record company's idiotic decision to release Phil's solo album a mere month before the release of Chinatown! Instead of releasing the album in the summertime the executives at Warner Brothers released Solo in Soho on September 17th, which turned out to be a complete bonehead move that confused fans and no doubt led to Chinatown's less than stellar reception one month later. Solo Peaked at #28 on the album charts but dropped into oblivion soon after.

People around during the time of the album didn't know what to make of it when they heard it and more than thirty years later new listeners are likely to get the same feeling. That's not to say it isn't any good, because as the case with all Lynott/Lizzy material there is no such thing as a truly bad album. It's just that Phil's hell raising rocker persona he had created for himself was nowhere to be found on his solo album. If Phil had actually taken the time to concentrate and focus on a true solo album without the distractions of heroin, touring and recording other albums at the same time, the results would have been no doubt spectacular. Jerome Rimson agrees, "Phil and his solo material could have been huge. The main downfall was that there was never enough time. He just took it as an aside as opposed to sitting down and writing songs with these people. If he had sat down with me and said I want to write some real r'n'b and soul music, we could have come up with some great stuff. Solo in Soho wasn't bad for a first showing considering that most of the songs were probably written in a day or two." Solo is frustrating as much as it is satisfying and showcases Phil's vast amount of musical range and versatility, so much that it's hard not to consider Phil one of the musical geniuses of the 20th century despite the album's half ass attempt at branching out and the uneven result it produced.

The most disappointing aspect of the album isn't the music, which had a host of all-star musical help and was extremely diverse going beyond the typical Lizzy sound formula, but surprisingly was the lyrics. Usually Phil's strong point that all of a sudden failed miserably to live up to the epic poetic standards Phil could easily obtain. The swift loss of his lyrical mastery might not have been noticed by Phil or the others around him during this time, but no doubt this shocking development now seen in hindsight was due to the results of his heroin addiction. His nonchalant lyrics are too relaxed and mostly wrapped up in his street Romeo persona that his charisma pulls off while the chinks in his amour begin to show as his once commanding voice slowly loses its zeal. That being said it's still worth listening to and of course provides some musical highlights and moods. Only two singles were issued the first and most Lizzy-like "Dear miss lonely hearts" peaked at #32 and soon dropped out of sight. Written in Nassau and Co-written with former Rainbow, Wild Horses and Dio bass player Jimmy Bain and later covered by doomed L.A. rockers Hanoi Rocks the song is pretty corny despite having a decent chorus.

The other single "Kings Call" didn't fare much better reaching only #35 and falling off the charts altogether four weeks later. Phil's lament to one of his idols Elvis Presley that featured Dire Straits frontman Mark Knopfler was another excellently filmed video that would have benefited with the help of MTV. The video was once again shot by Mallet and featured varying background shots of the King Elvis intercut with Phil, Brian and Mark on a makeshift stage and artsy black and white backstage footage featuring models portraying groupies. Knopfler's unmistakable guitar twangs are vintage Dire Straits and the song is actually pretty decent. It's ironic that Knopfler's groundbreaking hit single with the Dire Straits "Money for nothing" ushered in the video era and put MTV on the map five years after filming "Kings Call". By the time Sting uttered the songs famous intro "I want my MTV" Phil was completely washed up, strung out and sadly a year away from meeting his maker.

The rest of Solo plods on with the overly plush "A Child's Lullaby" a sequel to "Sarah" consisting of over the top strings and sugary melodies. "Lullaby" is followed by the wasted "Tattoo (giving it all up for love)" a song that blows a funky ass bassline and good chorus with subpar lyricism and drumming. Thankfully the album's title track "Solo in Soho" is a true gem and single-handedly makes you forget just how awful the first four songs are. A "clapped out whore" narrates the beginning of the song and from then on an epic reggae tune with awesome lyrics reminds everyone just how tremendous Phil could be on a track. With Snowy on the guitar, Brian on the drums and Phil playing the bass, moog and percussion, all helping to add to the atmosphere of Phil's squalid tale of a streetwalker and her john…

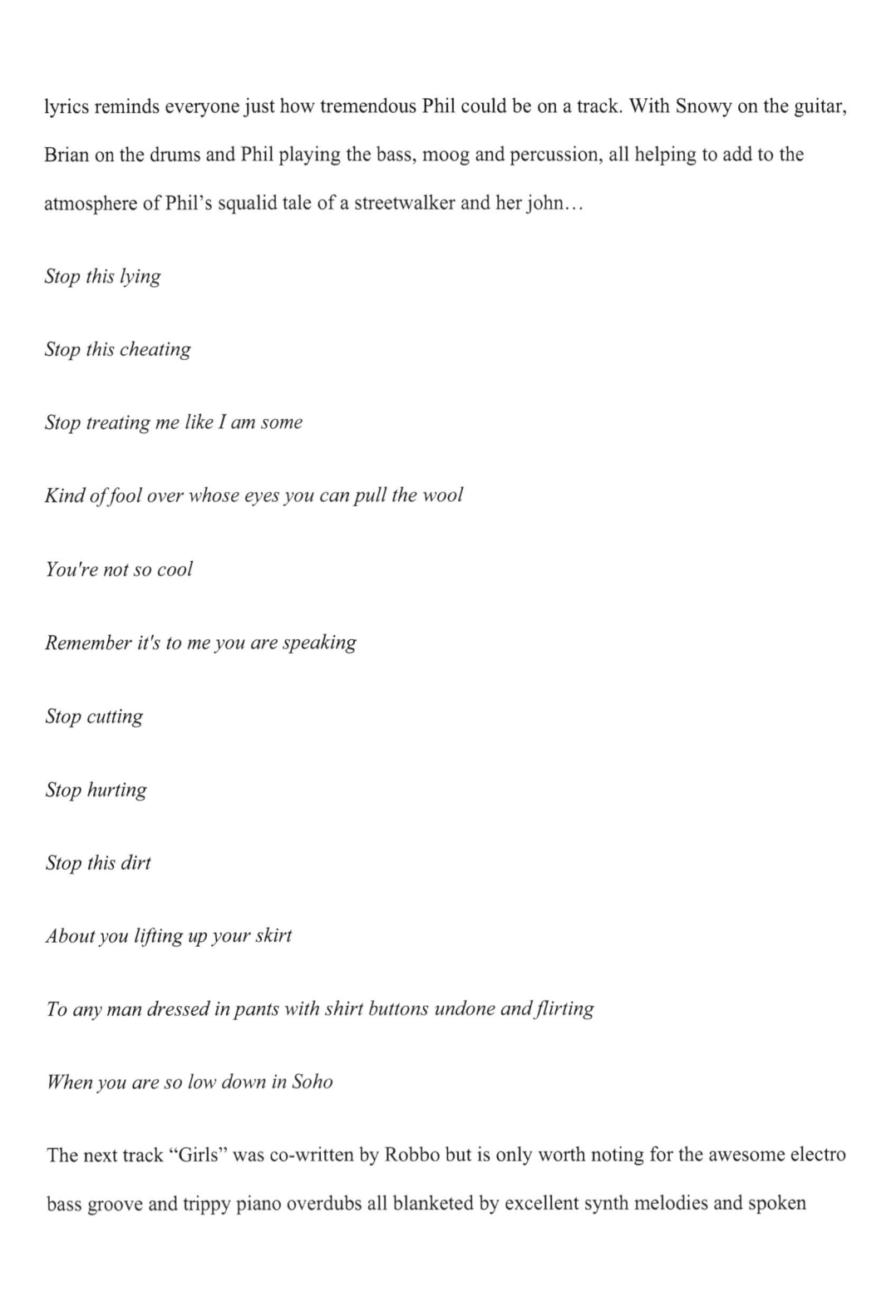

Stop this lying

Stop this cheating

Stop treating me like I am some

Kind of fool over whose eyes you can pull the wool

You're not so cool

Remember it's to me you are speaking

Stop cutting

Stop hurting

Stop this dirt

About you lifting up your skirt

To any man dressed in pants with shirt buttons undone and flirting

When you are so low down in Soho

The next track "Girls" was co-written by Robbo but is only worth noting for the awesome electro bass groove and trippy piano overdubs all blanketed by excellent synth melodies and spoken word female backing tracks. The song provides a perfect transition into the futuristic cut "Yellow Pearl" a song co-written by Midge Ure that a few years later served as the intro theme music on the revamped television show Top of the Pops. It's a stunning electro track and a pioneering work of the genre that was no doubt inspired by Phil's time working on the War of the Worlds, his fascination with robots and the coming totalitarian police state of spoke of in 1984. His lyrics were way ahead of their time…

It is foolish to venture into strange enchanted places

If they aren't the places you want to be

Attack, attack, attack, attack, attack, attack, attack

Is what we lack

We will arise

We will control

We will command

We will patrol

It is foolish under the guise of love and liberty

That we should capitalize and rob and fell

The poor for the socialistic tree

Phil explained how the song came about to Sounds on August 8, 1981:

That was nice. It was a throwaway thing that me and Midge put together as an experiment with electronics. Now that the sound has almost become passé and has gone on a stage further. The 'TOTP' thing was a compliment, these guys just came down and said they were looking for a new theme tune for the show and they fancied that track for it. This is two years after the song's been out.

Unfortunately, the rest of the album is unworthy filler with "Ode to a black man" "Jamaican rum" and "Talk in '79" barely worth listening to. Phil addressed the black issue with "Ode" getting it off his chest he told Sounds:

Yes with that I had had a long enough experience and that it was time for me to make a statement on the issue of the Black thing. All the time I was saying that I was Irish, but nothing about me being Black or at least not enough. The music industry is like 'hey we accept anybody, transvestites, blah blah blah', but only under certain conditions. In America they'll only accept Black Musicians if they'll play mindless Funk.

Despite Solo being a top 30 hit upon its initial release it would prove to be a total disappointment for Phil and the record company. Phil told the NME (which trashed an advanced copy of the album) what he thought of them in an interview on July 5th, 1980:

Like, I'll go on about the review in the NME of my album, because the guy reviewing it, he totally fucked up. He didn't know what he was talking about. He had it in for me, y'know? Because certain people had said I was the acceptable face of hard rock as far as the new wave was concerned - now, I never fucking gave myself that title. I've never been scared of the unknown. There was a time when punk was unknown and people went 'Well the guys can't play, he's not singing in tune, they're shit' and I went 'No, I like 'em'. There's nobody playing around, they've got energy which half the bands around today haven't got, they're playing short tight little numbers and they shock you into thinking.' And that appealed to me, but I wasn't jumping onto any bandwagon. Now this asshole for some reason seemed to think 'Right, he must think he's the fucking prophet here. I'll get him.' Now maybe I'm being totally wrong in my criticism of him, maybe I'm getting *him* arse about tit. But when he went for my album that was more on his mind than what he was listening to. 'Cos I read between the lines and the guy was a total fuckin' arse-hole. And if he had have said that to me face I would have stuck him out there and then. Simply because an insult is an insult, not criticism. Now that might be my narrow-mindedness, or a lack of seeing the other fella's point of view, but I don't see myself that way. I don't honestly think that I can be the leader of a band, an organization like Thin Lizzy, and not take into account other people's opinions. So I honestly feel that I do listen to criticism, other people's points of view, and bear them in mind and make a decision. [39]

While Phil's solo career was ending before it began, Thin Lizzy's eleventh album was approaching development hell with production delays and the air of uncertainty about what song would be their next single. Snowy had a leave of absence to fulfill contractual obligations to Pink Floyd and as the band assembled to film another video the stress had taken its toll. Booked on a return tour to Japan and Australia, Thin Lizzy gathered once again with David Mallet to film the video and promo pieces for their next single "Killer on the loose" which dropped on September 27th. The timing couldn't have been worse for a song based on Jack the Ripper, considering that a real life ripper was causing panic in London with a grisly string of murders. In the song Phil took on the persona of the ripper and it's possible that he even timed and planned the song to gain publicity while cashing in from the controversy of the Yorkshire ripper's murder spree. The song outraged women; especially feminists while the British press lauded the track as a gimmick. The song was intended to be controversial and it worked, landing like blood splatter at #10 proving that Thin Lizzy still had some fight left in them.

The equally offensive video was released to outrage a few months later and Phil drew ire from a furious press that bashed him for playing the role of Jack the ripper, dressed in a trench coat and surrounded by scantily clad vixens of the night. Although it was written as a warning to women taken out of context, the song became so controversial that radio stopped playing it and Lizzy was even forced to drop the song from their live set. The then state of the art video is interesting to watch for other reasons, mostly how noticeably bad Phil and Scott were starting to look, how bored Brian seemed to be and how utterly lost Snowy was in the context of the Thin Lizzy universe.

Thin Lizzy headed to Japan and rocked Tokyo while Chinatown was finally released on October 10th. It debuted at #11 and peaked at #7 before vanishing without grace less than three months later. As Lizzy began their downward spiral the realization of never having a number one album began to sink in and the numbing truth that they weren't getting any bigger dealt a devastating blow to the boys. Especially to Phil and Scott, forcing them to seek even more refuge in heroin to deal with this fact. No more singles were issued from Chinatown but the albums lead off track "We will be strong" should have been. It is an excellent anthem and kicks off the album with top-notch vocals from Phil matched with vintage Lizzy duel guitar melodies and catchy riffs to sonic sound perfection. The album's title track "Chinatown" is pure guitar heaven that sticks a knife in your gut and turns slowly, hurting so good that you sickly love it. This is Snowy White's greatest contribution to Lizzy as he shreds fire hot blues riffs that match Phil's sinister set of lyrics. Phil sings like a man who knows those Chinatown streets all too well and Brian's unsung groove shuffles us down those darkly lit roads. Although "Chinatown" barely missed being a top twenty hit in the UK it crapped out in America at a miserable #120 in December, putting the final nail in the coffin in Lizzy's dreams of ever again regaining their former Stateside glory.

Jim Fitzpatrick designed the Chinatown album cover, this time done in a completely new style that has gone on to become Lizzy's most iconic and popular work of cover art. It has molded the mainstream's view of Chinatown imagery and has appeared as tattoos on various people's bodies all across the world. It can't be understated how important Fitzpatrick's work was to Lizzy's legacy. Despite not providing any musical elements to the band, he was still without question a true member of Thin Lizzy. In a time when many bands turned to design houses like Hipgnosis, Thin Lizzy, was fortunate to have their own powerhouse design firm. Only he was one man, who just happened to be one of the greatest Irish artists of all time. Think about this as an example, Jim Fitzpatrick's most famous work was his simple two-tone portrait of Che Guevara. Jim turned Alberto Korda's famous 1960 picture of Che into one of the most iconic and copied posters in the world. Fitzpatrick's image of Che went viral and soon posters blanketed walls throughout in South America, on T-shirts and everywhere else in the civilized free world long before the modern exploits of Banksy. Jim's portrait of Che has become so commercialized that it can be found just as easily in the halls of the high-end fashion industry to hanging on the smoky walls of college dorms anywhere in the world. Despite managing this incredible artistic feat, it's doubtful that any design firms have ever paid Jim Fitzpatrick any royalties. Ireland's legendary artist even crossed paths with the infamous revolutionary who surprisingly had Irish ancestry:

Fitzpatrick even Jim met Che once, in 1961. The revolutionary poster boy dropped into a Kilkee pub on one of his Shannon stopovers between Cuba and the USSR. Jim was the barman. They chatted about the Irish diaspora to South America "and I was amazed he was so aware and proud of his Irish heritage". (His grandmother was a Galway Lynch.) In 2010, Jim reclaimed his copyright on his Che image, producing a limited edition print. He reveals: "I'm handing over all rights in perpetuity to the Cuban people via Che's daughter Aleida on the 27th of this month at Kilkee's Che do Bheatha Festival." He derides the "virulent campaign" of the US Right to smear him as glorifying a psycho killer. He retorts: "More people died here in 1916-21 than in the entire Cuban Revolution, so does that make Michael Collins or De Valera mass murderers?" [40]

The Chinatown album design especially the back of the album with its dragon face with vitrified glowing eyes has become so influential that even current Lizzy frontman Ricky Warwick had the artwork tattooed on his chest. Chinatown is actually Lizzy's closest attempt at successfully creating a concept album. From the inner vinyl record sleeves and possibly written by Phil:

CHINATOWN: The phenomenon of Chinatown occurs in many major cities in the West; recreating a small part of the Orient, wherever they spring into being. In old American western towns. Chinatown came into existence because of the large scale of immigration of cheap Chinese labor into the States during the building of the railroads. These areas have always been regarded with an element of suspicion and fear by Westerners; together with a curiosity and desire to indulge in the pleasures and vices which frequently seem to occur there, even to this day…This album was recorded in Chinatown in London. [41]

From an undated taped interview Phil gave that was played on the B.P. Fallon Show in 1983:

Chinatown is basically a blues kind of progression and that was it. And then there was the old Irish traditional line 'diddle-le diddle-le diddle-le diddle-le' and the rest was an arrangement that the band came up with, you know at the rehearsal, for example, a song like that would come along…I was working in 'Chinatown', you know. We were doing the album in Soho and I done 'Solo in Soho' there and I was in Chinatown everyday so…I was being influenced...I just thought, write lyrics about the seediness of the Chinatown area. I always found an association with misfits simply because, you know...Rock and Rollers, people in Rock and Roll are supposed to be misfits of society and stuff like that, so it's an affiliation. So when I was writing the lyrics of Chinatown when I was being influenced by... the dark side of all this, I thought I'd write about the people that don't survive in the rough part of Chinatown. I know there is a good side as well, but you know it's the evil side I use.[42]

The album continues full steam ahead as the third track "Sweetheart" is a brilliant guilty pleasure. It's a perfect blend of rock pop that Lizzy could do to perfection when all gears were firing. Phil's lyrics are political, social and personal and are some of the finest that he has ever written. When read below they really have an impact! "Sweetheart" is proof of how unique and special Thin Lizzy truly was and it should have been another hit single that scorched the American pop charts…

If I was to stand in a General Election

Would you tell me about your close inspection

And how I never stood for detection

Or would you take another man?

If I told you I had the solution to starvation

All the nations could be their own salvation

And those that lead us, lead us not into temptation

Or they pick another man?

(Sweetheart)

It's affecting

(Sweetheart)

It's so effective

(Sweetheart)

Do you detect in me?

(Sweetheart)

Sacred sweetheart

If I told you about my plan would you believe me?

This is my body, my blood, would you receive me?

Or would you be the first to deceive me

And take another man?

If I told you that I'm not the man to worry

Would you believe me when I said I was really sorry?

Or would you rush off in a hurry

To take another man?

Phil's sneaky nod to smack and cocaine "Sugar Blues" is a funky blues jam that Snowy lets loose on while Phil cranks out a thudding bassline. Brian's drums are good but by this point in his career he was basically on auto-pilot after shooting his wad on Black Rose. Scott and Snowy trade riffs well together on this track and it's a perfect gateway into the albums next cut the murderous "Killer on the Loose".

However it's all downhill from there as the rest of Chinatown is senseless filler. "Having a good time" could be the worst song Lizzy ever did and although "Genocide" rocks it's basically a substandard sequel to "Massacre." Representing a return to the American frontier in an effort to reclaim some stateside love the song is another epic ode to the original inhabitants of North America that got a raw deal. "Genocide" is Phil's hard rock Native redemption…

When they try to tell you knowledge is a dangerous thing

It's such a dangerous thing

The people that have it are the people that sin

And the people that need it are the people that can never win

They can never win Let me get you out of here little broken wing

There are people 'round here that are right

There are people 'round here that like to sleep at night

There are people 'round here that go slow

There are people 'round here

That don't take kindly to the killing of the buffalo

The final two tracks "Didn't I" a slow ballad that bores and "Hey you" a decent song about the dangers of leaving home for the big city and the false illusions of having it made, round out an album that Greg Prato of Allmusic rightfully called a "letdown" especially compared to their previous album the stellar Black Rose. Longtime Lizzy manager Chris O'Donnell wasn't a fan of Chinatown either calling it, "Absolute garbage, and when Phil brought in a keyboard player for Renegade, that was it for me," summing up emphatically, "a once brilliant band was turning into a pile of crap before my eyes." Paul du Noyer traveled with Phil from Glasgow to Liverpool and wrote about Thin Lizzy's eventual undoing for the NME on July 5th, 1980:

Gone are the days when NME writers used to routinely return from assignments with Philip Lynott complete with back-slapping anecdotes of casual camaraderie and amiable banter. Since those halcyon times of 'Jailbreak' in 1976, when the boys were back in triumph and Thin Lizzy reached twin peaks of popularity and prestige, measures of suspicion and disillusionment have set in on both sides. Successive releases of recent years have met with the now familiar allegations of stagnation and decline in Lizzy's creative powers - and by implication in those of

Lynott himself. A while ago, the process culminated in the comprehensive trashing handed out in these very pages to his long-awaited 'Solo In Soho' set. In the few days I spent with Philip Lynott - traveling, drinking, seeing the band in action - it wasn't difficult to sense the reserve that typifies his relations with potential critics now. For my part, I came away with the image of a group that's far from finished, but one which works more on the principle of efficiency than on that of risk. And to spend time inside such a successful, large scale enterprise – a livelihood for far more than four people - is to wonder if it's merely naive to expect anything different. Lynott takes his responsibilities seriously - to the Thin Lizzy organization which depends upon him, to the unswervingly loyal following on which he ultimately depends, to his family. And the pressures are not enviable. Out in public - on the stage, in the hotel bar, the radio talk-in - Lynott can assume the familiar roles like an old overcoat. It seems to keep everyone happy, and he seems to enjoy it. But the private Lynott is a much more complex proposition. And nearly impossible to know. The modern Philip Lynott interview, he'll imply, is not an occasion for soul-baring. It's for publicity. We sat in a disheveled hotel room that overlooked the Liverpool skyline - soot-black clusters of Victorian chimney pots, landmarks, seagulls.

Phil wearily talks about Chinatown as he takes a sip from his beer:

At worst it'll be the same. People will say 'Another Thin Lizzy album' like previous albums. People are just going to say 'When are the band going to do something different, blah blah blah.' I figure that's the way it'll go at worst. But at best I think there'll be a whole new lease of energy, because I've got a lot of the softer things that used to slip into a Lizzy album out of me system with the solo album. We're always caught with this paradox that we don't change quick enough for the people who are reviewing us, and yet we change too quickly for the people who are paying to see the concerts - and somewhere in between is where the band's heart lies. It's the paradox of success: the reviewers are always waiting for us and we'll be trying to show the audience that there's more to us than just old hits.[43]

By October Lizzy was back on the road promoting the ill-fated album from half a world away in Japan and Australia. Their first show in Sydney turned comically disastrous as their PA system erupted and blew holes through the roof while fire sparks scorched Snowy's chest. Nobody was seriously hurt and a few hours later they got back to business and grinded out their set. Back in England by November, the band prepped for their final American tour while preparing songs and ideas for the bands next obligated studio project. Phil's American swan song was a disaster as Chinatown barely made the top 200. Scott had problems of his own and his drug habits caused him to dislocate his knee before a gig in D.C., forcing him to continue the tour hip deep in plaster while sitting on a stool during Lizzy's remaining shows. It didn't last long as Scott left the tour to spend time with his family in California during the Christmas holidays while the rest of Lizzy canceled the lackluster gigs and headed back across the Atlantic. It would be the final time that Phil would rock America and the memories were bittersweet and gut-wrenchingly disappointing.

Back home Phil was grilled by studio executives, now weary of his visually evident drug habits not to repeat the results of the doomed efforts of Chinatown. The album was a marketing nightmare and without the support of Warner Brothers it quickly faded from the charts and into Lizzy folklore as the beginning of the end. At the start of 1981, Phil and the gang flew back to Compass Point studios in the Bahamas to begin work on his second solo album. By the time they returned home a few weeks later the boys were looking the worse for wear and the lackluster response and dwindling crowds during the Chinatown tour took a huge emotional toll on them.

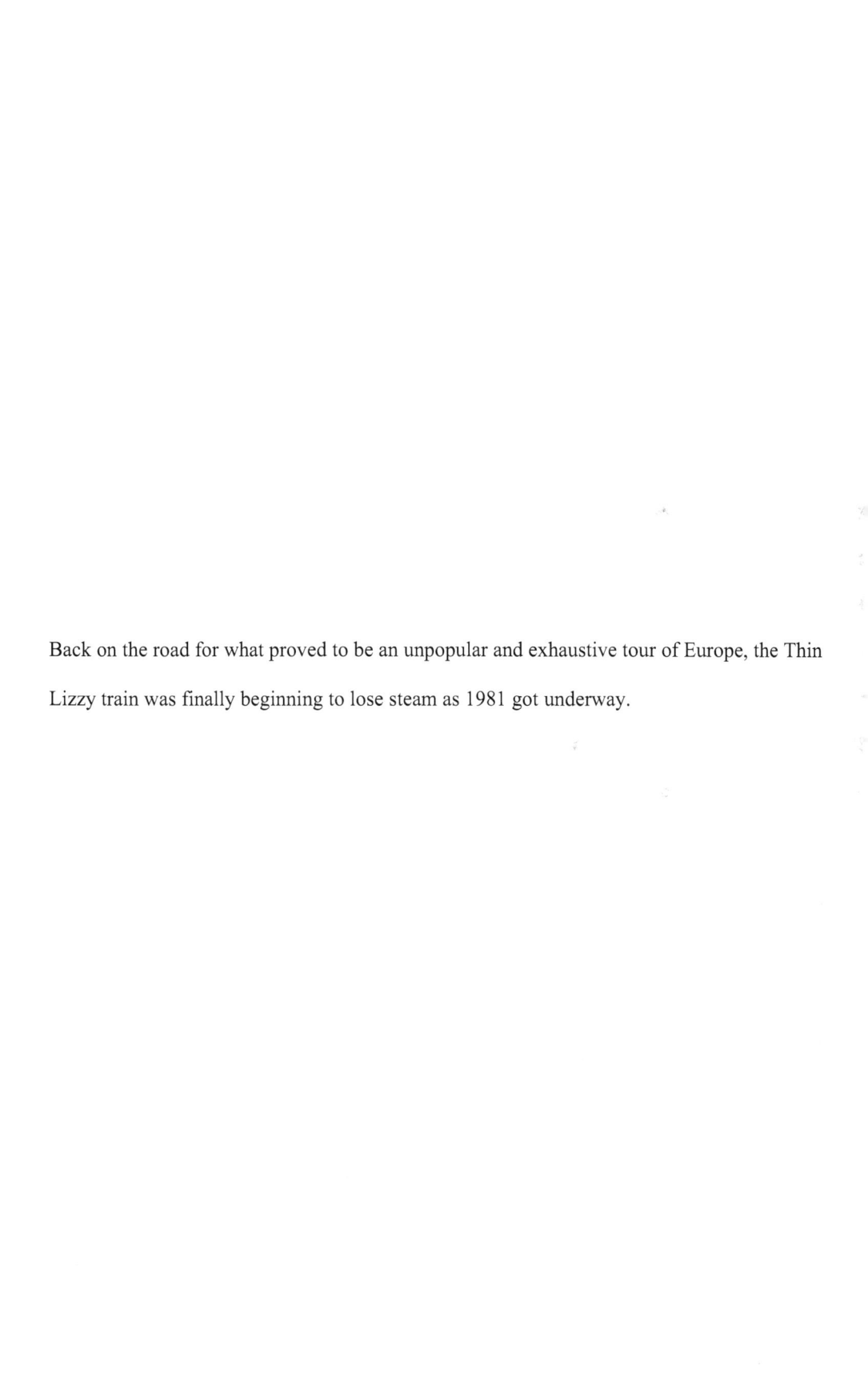

Back on the road for what proved to be an unpopular and exhaustive tour of Europe, the Thin Lizzy train was finally beginning to lose steam as 1981 got underway.

It's getting Dangerous

Right well I knew when I set sail

What my fate would be

When gazing on my native hills

They seemed to fly from me

I watched them as they wore away

Until my eyes grew sore

Well knowing I was doomed to tread

On shamrock soil no more

Samuel "The Renegade" Blair

After the disastrous affair of the Chinatown tour, Phil and the boys were once again back in the recording studio. And similar to the recordings that took place the previous year, they were once again shuffling through vast amounts of half-ass material from another Phil solo effort and the next untitled Lizzy album. Phil wasn't satisfied with the results of his first solo album and began work on the follow up Fatalistic Attitude almost immediately. The problem of course was that his drug habit worsened and the album was done in the exact same manner as his previous ones, with a bunch of backing musicians and Lizzy members working on stuff that nobody knew what album it would be appearing on.

Thin Lizzy was burnt out and disillusioned when they began work on their twelfth studio album Renegade at Morgan studios in London. Phil hired another promising young producer/sound engineer Chris Tsangarides to help assist with the enviable task of recording a Thin Lizzy album. Phil was desperate to get back on the charts and at the same time had grown fond of Darren Wharton's keyboard skills and the advancements made in synthesizer sound development. He wanted to expand the Lizzy sound and felt that Tsangarides was young and hip enough to be on the current trends of the music industry. Phil was right as Thin Lizzy unknowingly began to branch out into heavy metal territory while the rest of the world was caught in the post-punk new wave landscape and Tsangarides was the man that made it possible.

Chris Tsangarides got his start working with Judas Priest in 1975 and would later go on to produce more albums from metal legends including Anvil, Helloween, Angra, Tygers of Pantang, Black Sabbath, King Diamond, Bruce Dickinson, and guitar virtuoso Yngwie Malmsteen. Tsangarides would eventually cross into pop production working with Tom Jones and Depeche Mode, culminating in a career that saw him nominated for a Grammy award in 1991. But ten tears earlier Chris was asked to help out flustering Lizzy producer Kit Woolven to try and make sense to the band's current mess of recordings. These scattered recordings took place until June and much like Chinatown the bands previous effort, Renegade which still hadn't had a title was left discarded and in shambles sitting on the shelf until the record company or

Lizzy could figure out what to do with it. Snowy White would later recall that the sessions for Lizzy and Phil's solo albums were so messy that he should have been paid as a session player.

While the confusion lingered about the bands next album so did the choice of their next single issued to commemorate the release of Thin Lizzy's first Greatest Hits album. The single "Trouble Boys" was released as a standalone to their 'hits' album The Adventures of Thin Lizzy released in April. The song "Trouble Boys" a tune that nobody in the band except Phil wanted as a single was an epic flop that barely reached #53 and was the bands worst charting single since 1975. The album fared much better peaking at #6 on the UK album charts. Mostly because the album cover and accompanying inlay was a brilliant Marvel inspired comic book adaptation done once again by Jim Fitzpatrick. Showing the renegades Lizzy depicted as cowboys and outlaws in the wild, wild, west it is another example of how unique and cutting edge a Thin Lizzy album could be. The fans appreciated the warm collection of classic Lizzy tunes and stunning new panels of art to trip on and responded by giving Thin Lizzy another gold record to add to their mantle.

To promote the album Lizzy committed to a series of festival gigs. Starting the tour off with small warm up shows in the Channel Islands of Jersey and Guernsey and then onto a disastrous performance at the Milton Keynes bowl. A show faced with torrential downpours, a sparse crowd, non-rocking opening acts and bad smack. They regained their form during the Scottish stretch of the tour and returned to Dublin to rock the Slane Castle festival, proving once again that when Thin Lizzy were on, they were still a force to be fucking reckoned with. The bands arrival in a helicopter was epic Thin Lizzy showmanship that instantly got the crowd fired up.

While back in Dublin Phil went to court over a drugs charge that had been issued against him in 1979. The fuzz tricked their way into Phil's Kew road home by posing as gas workers and discovered a few bits of marijuana and cocaine, along with a few weed plants. The charges were eventually dropped after Phil paid a £200 fine and magically Phil managed to keep the police far away from his stash, even though it was pretty obvious that by the summer of 1981, Phil was a full-blown junkie. In late August Thin Lizzy played the Rockpalast in a live television performance broadcast in Germany and then promptly canceled their remaining UK gigs and returned back to London to put the finishing touches on their twelfth and still untitled album. While the fall leaves turned and Lizzy chipped away in the studio the press started reporting that Phil was in negotiations to play Jimi Hendrix in a screen adaption of the iconic rockers life. Jimi was one of Phil's hero's and he was genuinely excited to have a crack at playing him. Phil even got together again with Eric Bell and Brian Downey to record a monster tribute song to commemorate Hendrix's ten-year death anniversary in 1980. Unfortunately the Phil playing Hendrix bio project never happened. Phil was even offered other small bits in movies and television shows that never came to pass either, likely due to the ravished state that the heroin abuse was beginning to have on his body and appearance.

As the fall of 1981 deepened they still couldn't find a good enough title for the new album that was close to being finished. Wanting some fresh air Phil left the studio and walked towards the nearest watering hole. He stopped for traffic and watched a motorcycle slowly ride by him. On the back of the bikers vest was a patch of the Thin Lizzy logo and beside the logo were the words Renegade. Phil snapped his fingers in a eureka moment and bolted back to the studio to tell Tsangarides that he finally had the name of the album and the inspiration for a new song, which he immediately started penning.

Renegade was released in November without a lead single and quickly tripped over itself into oblivion, reaching #38 in the UK and #157 in America. It featured a strange cover depicting a red flag with a star in the upper right-hand corner, instead of the center, which would have made it sympathetic with the Chinese. It totally doesn't make sense at all, especially the back cover that shows each band member holding this flag. Renowned rock photographer Denis O'Regan staged the bizarre photo shoot at his London studio. To make matters worse keyboardist Darren Wharton, who was a full member of the band by this time and contributed greatly to the album was left out of the group picture. The record company screwed up big time and had such little faith or interest in the album that it's no wonder Renegade sank into Lizzy mythology as a discarded side note in the bands discography. Renegade is even considered by fans and the media as their worst album. Although not terrible the album is weak when compared to their previous eleven outings, but interesting because it represents an expanded and different, albeit less heavy sound. Lizzy were branching out in metal territory and Phil's sound was growing with the added depth of a keyboard player, a vital element that would have a major presence in the overall sound of 80's music. Like Hendrix before him wanting to expand in jazz and rock fusion, Phil was also branching out musically, which makes sense because after all Phil had been doing music basically his whole life, even the rocker must have eventually gotten bored at times.

With Renegade Phil began to lay the groundwork for what Lizzy might have sounded in the 80's and the album's opening track is a stunner. "Angel of Death" is pure metal cheese despite Scott saying it, "Was too heavy metal for words, and I hated it. I mean, how much more corn do you want? There were great big hunks of butter dripping of that sucker!" Scott's opinion notwithstanding "Angel" is darkly epic and very musical, co-written by Wharton, who adds excellent synth soundscapes and an ominous mood. The track features great storytelling, heavy guitar riffs and pounding drums with Halloween themed shakers. Phil's narration is a bit silly and mostly unintelligible, but the track works simply because of the apocalyptic theme and the current love affair of all things prophetic and conspiratorial. Phil had just read the Prophecies of

Nostradamus, a new age book about a 16th-century French prophet that supposedly foresaw the future doomed events of mankind. Inspired by Nostradamus's trippy ass poetry, Phil penned "Angel of Death" in the French bard's honor, telling BBC Radio 1 that, "The idea for the song came when I was reading the 'Prophecies of Nostradamus'. It's a very popular book in France now. Recently its sales have picked up because of the Cold War. He said that an 'Angel of Death' would come and create a holocaust which everybody considers to be a nuclear war."

The next song is the album's title track "Renegade" and it stops the metal induced mania of the opener. It's slow, boring, horribly sung by Phil and utterly miscalculated filler. The lyrics about a lonely biker are far better than Phil's weak vocal performance…

He's just a boy that his lost his way

He's a rebel that has fallen down

He's a fool been blown away

To you and me he's a renegade

He's a clown that we put down

He's a man that doesn't fit

He's a king but not in this town

To you and me he's a renegade

But he is a king when he's on his own

He's got a bike and that's his throne

And when he rides he's like the wind

To you and me he's a renegade

The albums third track, penned by Phil and Scott, "The Pressure Will Blow" finally shows that some life was still left in the heavy shredding rockers. Phil growls with intensity and fires shots at the record label, his wife, drug dealers, the fans, so called friends and critics. Thin Lizzy was in a downward spiral and looking for a way out of the musical hellhole they'd dug so deep for themselves. Phil was stuck in a rut, creatively and physically; his fleeting shot at fame and getting back to Lizzy's Jailbreak peak was now unreachable. The "Pressure" is a sincere confrontation of those failures and the post traumatic effects of being successful but never again tasting that exact same elixir. The song rocks, especially the duel guitar harmony breakdown and Phil's gut punching lyrics…

Set me on my destination

Point me the way to my position

What's the meaning of my mission?

I have made my decision clear

I don't need another reason

I don't want any more prime time

I have made my decision

Not for the first but for the last time

I'm settin' on slow

I'm buildin' it up

I'm lettin' it go

The pressure will blow on time

Renegade's fourth song is a straight up rip off of ZZ Top. Phil even admits so! Following the ZZ Top rip off is without a doubt the best song on the album and a scorcher that single handily proved that despite the unevenness or vast amount of musical style experimenting Thin Lizzy has never made a bad album. "Hollywood (down on your luck)" is a classic song that combines the finest of what Thin Lizzy had to offer. Excellent lyrics and storytelling with deep insightful poetic themes matched with virtuoso musical arrangements. The true tragedy of this song is that Lizzy's record company failed to shoot a video for it! It would have been a great addition to the then blooming MTV and no doubt helped the single move some copies. With the label abandoning the song it sank at #53 on the UK charts, but to everyone's surprise it managed to land at #24 on the American rock charts, but with no support or video "Hollywood" soon dropped out of public eye and into the crowded bag of unpolished gems that litter Thin Lizzy's vaults.

After "Hollywood" the Renegade album pretty much slips into a coma. "No one told Him" is a weak song that sounds suspiciously like "Dear Miss Lonely Hearts" and "Fats" just doesn't belong on a Thin Lizzy album. It's not a bad song, and Wharton definitely deserves praise for his awesome keyboard playing, that being said it just doesn't fucking rock and is more suited for a smoky little jazz club somewhere in the Village. Song number eight on the Renegade album is the wasted "Mexican Blood" another nod to classic Americana but despite some great acoustic Spanish guitar work it is a total clunker based on a now tired theme. The albums closer "It's Getting Dangerous" is another hidden gem a bit of morbid soul-searching realness co-written by Scott. He and Phil get deep as it becomes abundantly clear to what they're talking about. The star-crossed rockers were completely knee deep in the hard drugs and way over their heads. With declining health, dwindling crowds and record sales "It's Getting Dangerous" is one of the finest songs ever created on the subject of lost youth and how best friends can easily go their separate ways. Phil's lyrics are astounding and complimented by excellent music arrangements of pounding drums, synth stabs doubled over drum echoes, great keyboard layering, top-notch guitar melodies and breakdowns. Phil even does his best singing on the album and the chorus is fantastically touching.

Now who in the world would believe

That he's got another trick up his sleeve

And who in the world wants to know

Which way should he go

Which way should he turn?

Which way should he learn?

Which day should he stop?

Which way to the top?

I remember him when we were friends

When we were young, way back then

I still can recall when we were small

How he tried his best to warn us all

This living on his own has turned his heart

To stone and it's all pain

He sits out on his own and eats his heart

Out alone in the pouring rain

Now who in the world would have known

That just a few years ago

His love could have grown and grown

Through the rain, the sleet and snow

But the rain, the sleet and snow

Chills the heart and kills the soul

So let the cold winds blow

What he doesn't see, he doesn't know

I remember him when we were friends

When we were young, way back then

I recall it all when we were small

How he tried his best to warn us all

I remember it still, I always will

When we were friends way back then

I recall it all when we were small

How he tried his best to warn us all of the danger

He said, "Watch out for the danger"

He said, "Watch out"

The man is a winner for the first time in his life

He looks a little thinner but he says, "Hey that doesn't matter"

But if you look closely you'll see

A cold smug self-satisfactory smile behind

And now that he has won

It doesn't matter how or which way it was done

Now that he's in control

Revenge is in his heart and soul

The power is at his fingertips

Vengeance is on his lips

But the power he fought to control

Now has got him in its grips

I remember him when we were friends

When we were young, way back then

I recall it all when we were small

How he tried his best to warn us all

I remember it still, I always will

When we were friends way back then

I recall it all when we were small

How he tried his best to warn us all of the danger

I remember him when we were friends

When we were young, way back then

But now we're all grown up

And we're strangers

You see, bit by bit, part by part

We slipped and slipped

Till we'd grown apart

And now we're strangers

The Renegade album failed to spark enthusiasm with the critics or the fans and without a single to promote it dropped out of sight after peaking at #38 on the UK album charts. The consensus among critics was that Thin Lizzy had their day and it was now time to step aside and let the young pretenders have a go at the big time. By the middle of November, Lizzy were back on tour and fighting for their musical lives. Their star was on the wane and much like Gary Moore before him, a disgusted Snowy White quit the band rather than to stick around and watch Phil and Scott's spiraling drug problems turn the musical swashbucklers Thin Lizzy into a sad self-parody of epic proportions.

Snowy quit the band shortly after the Renegade tour wrapped up and made his last appearance in the rock documentary Renegade: The Philip Lynott Story produced by RTE. Shot by David Heffernan between London and Ireland over a period of six weeks, the doc was meant to boost the dismal sales of Renegade and show the Lizzy members in a formal tea-sipping atmosphere for the first time. It was also the first real in-depth documentary about Phil's life, the formation of Lizzy, their influences and what the Irish rockers were able to accomplish musically and commercially in thirteen years. It contained lots of live footage, promo videos and Snowy's last visual appearance with Lizzy during a jam session taped at Phil's Kew Road garage. The film was more of a commercial for a free falling band than anything else.

With Snowy White's departure, Thin Lizzy was once again facing life without a twin guitar to compliment Scott and the trademarked Thin Lizzy sound. The only difference this time was Phil and Scott seemed more worried about where they were going to get their next fix of heroin instead of another guitarist. As Scott told VH1's Behind the Music so blatantly, "The great Thin Lizzy goal all of a sudden now it started to feel like it wasn't achievable any longer. And if it was, I wondered if I even cared."

In late January, the Renegade tour continued its disastrous run when a bouncer in Aarhus, Denmark fucked up Brian Downey to the extreme of sending him to the hospital. With one look at Brian's engorged face, Lizzy management decided to send him back home to Ireland. Brian the silent dependable one who always had his shit together was so bored by the tour and disgusted at Phil and Scott's growing smack addiction. To conquer this frustration he turned to alcohol more and more until his drunken mouth wrote a check his ass couldn't cash resulting in an old fashioned pummeling at the pub. Filling in for Brian once again was drummer Mark Nauseef, who thankfully for Lizzy was opening up for them during the tour with the Look-a-likes. Thin Lizzy plodded on through gigs in Sweden and Norway before returning to Ireland in February, where a recuperated Brian joined them to rock Whitla Hall in Belfast. The Renegade tour continued on to France and Spain but by the time it hit Portugal, Scott's body finally shut down and he collapsed. Strung out and rendered unable to perform, Scott's exhaustion (heroin withdrawals) sent him back to England to recover while Lizzy marched on as a four-piece to Germany. When they returned to London Phil promptly canceled a number of British dates and the rest of the band took a break while Phil returned to the studio to finish his second solo album. Alan Byrne described the tumultuous start of the year Lizzy was facing:

As 1982 kicked in, so did the drugs. Out of the charts, and rather frequently out of their minds on stage, Thin Lizzy was faltering, and faltering fast. Husband and father of two, Lynott sat down and tried vainly to rescue what was left of his reputation and that of his position in the rock world. Re-assessing his marriage would come later, but for now he found himself bereft of inspiration, and he turned once more to the splintered cushion of hard drugs. Scott Gorham too had been dabbling with heroin, and both he and Lynott would live out the remainder of their Lizzy lives in a drug-induced rage. Rage at the fact that they could no longer command the large audiences – the fact that the band didn't seem to be getting as big as they foresaw. It was in this frame of mind that Thin Lizzy began 1982, and with another schedule packed with tour dates the performances and sheer power of Thin Lizzy began to fade. [43]

By the summer, Phil had completed his second solo album and was touring Ireland to promote it. He hired an all-star group of musicians to support him and this set would become known as the Philip Lynott Soul Band. It was the exact opposite of a Lizzy experience; Phil was laid back and a crooner, his Romeo image played to perfection when he wasn't too stoned to pull it off. It was a series of relaxed shows that had intimate jam sessions and reworking's of a few Lizzy hits alongside a bunch of Phil's solo material. During the tour the label released the albums lead single "Together" but it failed to chart.

Shocked but unfazed Phil continued to pour his heart out during his solo tour but unfortunately most of the fans had lost interest. Making the year worse was the burning down of Philomena's Manchester Hotel in July. Phil and his mother lost a lot of family photographs and sentimental objects and were both devastated by the unfortunate event. A month later Snowy officially quit the band in Castlebar after an argument with a stoned Phil about the bands recent pathetic performances. Shortly after Snowy's exit, long time Lizzy co-manager Chris O'Donnell also walked away in disgust from the once great Thin Lizzy. Chris told VH1 years later that, "Here's a guy whose role models were all dead rock stars. Hendrix, Elvis, Janis Joplin, Brian Jones, they're all dead. He knew that it is a great possibility if you live a single lifestyle, and model yourself on those icons, that quite possibly your end will be the same." The world came crashing down on the boys at the precise moment they were obligated to enter the studio to deliver their 13th album - an unlucky number for an unlucky band.

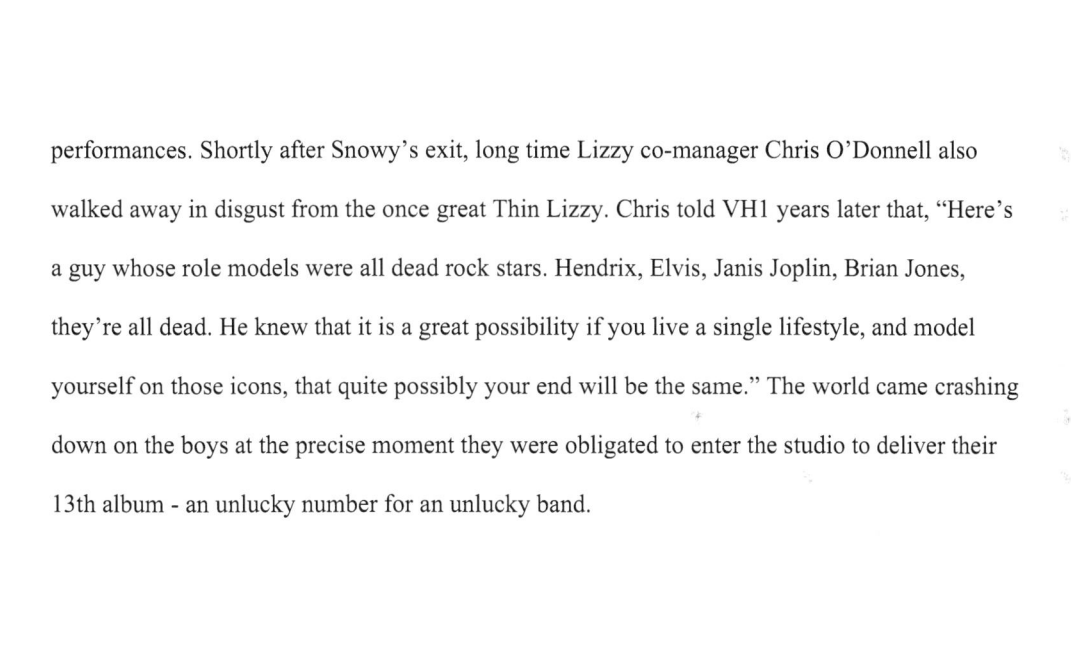

Ride the Lightning

A man there came, whence none could tell

Bearing a Touchstone in his hand

And tested all things in the land

By its unerring spell

Quick birth of transmutation smote

The fair to foul, the foul to fair

Purple nor ermine did he spare

Nor scorn the dusty coat

Of heirloom jewels, prized so much

Were many changed to chips and clods

And even statues of the Gods

Crumbled beneath its touch

Then angrily the people cried

'The loss outweighs the profit far; our goods suffice us as they are

We will not have then tried

And since they could not so prevail

To check this unrelenting guest, they seized him, saying –

'Let him test how real it is, our jail!

But, though they slew him with the sword

And in a fire his Touchstone burn'd

Its doings could not be o'erturned

Its undoings restored

And when to stop all future harm

They strew'd its ashes on the breeze

They little guess'd each grain of these

Convey'd the perfect charm

North, south, in rings and amulets

Throughout the crowded world 'tis borne

Which, as a fashion long outworn

In ancient mind forgets

William Allingham

Without a guitarist to play off Scott, and Scott being in no condition to be reliable with coming up with the majority of the riffs Thin Lizzy had a major problem. Without White and scheduled to begin recording their next album soon things were looking bleak for the duel guitar sound that had already grown stale. During August Lynott stopped by Dunbar Studios in London to share a smoke with friend and producer Chris Tsangarides who was working on a session with the fresh guitar hero named John Sykes. Like Robbo before him, Sykes was the young guitar virtuoso that Lizzy needed to pump the life back into its listless body. Phil was impressed immediately upon meeting the kid and called Brian and Wharton to come in and play on Sykes' single "Please don't Leave me" while Phil sang lead. Released by MCA, the ballad flopped despite heavy promotion.

Sykes an ex-member of the early metal band Tygers of Pan Tang soon found a new home with Lizzy as he was made an official member and joined Lizzy at Eel Pie Studios in London by early September. Sykes contributed such guitar ferocity to the first two Tygers albums that when Ozzy Osbourne heard Sykes left the band, Ozzy gave him an immediate audition. Sykes lost the job to the legendary Randy Rhodes. Sykes would also have more musical bad luck after co-writing the massive hit "Is this love" with David Coverdale for the Whitesnake self-titled album and then getting fired before it shot to #2 on the American album charts. The Whitesnake album on which Sykes got shafted moved 8 million records and Coverdale's ridiculously awesome mane and power vocals redefined 80's metal videos.

Phil's second solo album kept getting delayed and the suits at the record label forced Phil to change the title of the album from Fatalistic Attitude to anything else. Out of ideas, Phil settled on the ridiculously lame The Philip Lynott Album and prepared to shoot a video for the next single "Old Town" a song that in time would rank as a high mark in Phil's life. Ironically the incredible video and single failed to make a dent on the charts and was considered a disappointment upon its release. The now classic video features the actress Fionna Mckenna and was shot in Dublin over two days by director Gerry Gregg and producer Dave Heffernan. The video is epic and showcases Phil in classic Dublin spots like Grafton Street, The Long Hall, Herbert Park, Ringsend Pier and of course iconic shots of him struttin' over Ha'Penny bridge. When "Old Town" failed to chart and the record company (showing little interest in the project) rejected the album cover artwork and delayed the release of the album until September, Phil almost crumbled in disbelief. Once again retreating to the needle and the spoon.

A few days later he walked along the beach with Jim Fitzpatrick and played him a cassette of the album from a Sony Walkman. Jim couldn't believe what he heard bursting out of the over-sized 80's suction cup headphones. Fitzpatrick recalled:

I was simply blown away by what I heard. I couldn't believe the record company didn't like it. At this point I knew Philip was in trouble, he could take neither the rejection of his artistry nor the crap that went with it. We walked on for another couple of hours and I could sense a desperate sadness coming from deep inside him, presumably he was experiencing a great sense of failure. The man I met that day was disillusioned and cynical about his profession, "running on empty" he called it.[44]

The Philip Lynott Album was dead on arrival after being released on September 17th, 1982 as it failed to chart and put the kibosh on Phil's attempt to broaden his image outside of the Thin Lizzy brand. Despite the strong presence of "Old Town" Phil's second solo album was a huge flop, and its only saving grace was the remixed version of "Yellow Pearl" which went to #14 on the singles charts and got picked up as the theme music for Top of the Pops. The album featured some awful elements of 80's production styles and at times resembled a night at the disco gone horribly awry. Most of the tracks are tired and basic affairs that slant towards trivial imitations of pop, disco, funk and reggae, with plenty of cushy ballads thrown in for good measure.

The album's music is pretty decently composed but lacks the compliment of great songwriting due to Lynott's creative talents being eaten away by drug abuse. Phil's lyrical output, always his strong point was now for the first time coming out hackneyed and uninspired. Another concern was the quality of Lynott's singing, his voice now gravelly and lacking any conviction, sounding like a former crooner that lost his voice to bags of dope. The album opener "Fatalistic Attitude is a downer about depression and suicide. The next track "The Mans a Fool" is a funky disco number that borders on Xanadu inspired cheese. "Old Town" rescues the album for a brief moment but the next cut the obligatory nod to Phil's second daughter "Cathleen" is a slow ballad with a harmonica solo from Huey Lewis. "Growing Up" is another boring ballad written in the third person that illustrates to the audience how his or your little girls might grow up. The sixth track on The Philip Lynott Album was the remixed hit "Yellow Pearl" a song that got Phil back in the British top twenty. An out of shape Phil shot an MTV worthy video for the song, full of cutting edge technologic wonders (a walkman!) silhouetted by synthesizers and hot Asian beauties. Although it's unclear what the video has to do with the song lyrics, Phil explained to the B.P. Fallon Rock show in Dublin on October 10th, 1982 how "Yellow Pearl" became the theme song for Top of the Pops:

It was funny because the people from 'Top of the Pops' for some reason the producer of the show really liked the song and he came up to me and he said would I write the new theme music for 'Top of the Pops'. So we're in the studio and I'm sort of sayin' 'What do you want? What type of song are you looking for?' and he went 'something like this Yellow Pearl' and I said 'Why don't you use Yellow Pearl?' and he went 'Good Idea!' When I first recorded it, the version you played there is the second version that was released. When I first recorded it there was no drums. And then they decided to release it as a single so we put some drums on it and we got Rusty Egan from 'Visage' and he played drums on it and we released it and it went nowhere. Of course when 'Top of the Pops' used it as a theme song, they decided to re-release it again. So, if first you don't have a hit, release it again! We did a remix of it again. The final mix is the best mix and the way you can tell that is that it doesn't have the girl's voice in the start and it's a much better mix. But anyway, it did well...and then it was on that album 'Action Tracks' as well, so it made me a fortune. Every time I see 'Top of the Pops' the cash register in me head rings.[45]

Following "Yellow" is the funk number "Together" a tune that failed to chart but with Midge's groovy drum machine work and an inspired bassline from Jerome Rimson you can't help but shake your groove thing upon hearing it. Phil even had it mixed with heavy drum and bass and pressed up 12" vinyl's for the disco disc jockeys. The hard rocking Lizzy front man had now gone disco and the fans that couldn't learn to separate the two were at a lost to explain just what the fuck was going on. Phil wasn't concerned saying, "I think the Lizzy supporters are very capable of liking two styles of music from the same artist. The reason I'm keen to keep my own thing going as well is because I write an abundance of material that I want to put out."

The eighth song on the album "Little Bit of Water" is a unique track that features excellent keyboard work from Wharton and Phil playing an Irish harp to angelic perfection. It has a great melody, and cool tin drums but lacks any sort of lyrical depth. Apparently it's about Phil being married but the repetitive chorus and lackadaisical singing ruin what could have been a stellar track. The album's woes continue with "Ode to Liberty (The Protest Song)" a song with some killer Mark Knopfler riffs that a mumbling Phil ruins with his inept vocals. The last two songs on the album are "Gino" and "Don't talk About Me Baby" two pointless fillers that should have remained on the recording studio shelf. Phil was much better than the drivel compiled on the The Philip Lynott Album and it's no surprise that the album was declared an epic disaster before falling off the face of the earth shortly after being released.

A Disenchanted Phil returned to Eel Pie studios in November to finish recording Thin Lizzy's final album Thunder and Lightning. With the overdubs finished at the Record Plant a month later the boys were shocked upon hearing the mastered version of the album. John Sykes had provided Lizzy with a Van Halen tinged spark of renewed excitement and the album came out sounding heavier than anything they had done in years. In fact it came out sounding as the heaviest album Thin Lizzy ever made! It was metal as fuck and laid new bridges to cross for a whole new generation of young up and coming musicians. It was the first truly influential heavy metal album and Phil, Scott, Brian, and Darren Wharton all had a sudden bolt of renewed combustible energy thanks to the inspired shredding of guitar whiz kid John Sykes. And with Tsangarides' pioneering metal production skills Thunder and Lightning was bound to replant the hard rocking flag that Lizzy used to proudly fly sky high. Tsangarides and Sykes helped pull Thin Lizzy out of the '70s and into the dawn of the metal age. As Christmas approached the members of Thin Lizzy were fully re-energized and completely sold that their new album was their best work in years. They made plans for a tour to support the album and buzz grew in music circles that once again Thin Lizzy was back. But the recent addition of guitarist John Sykes hadn't provided the outcome they desired and as the gig dates approached in late January of 1983 the ticket sales were appalling. Horrified with the lack of sales plus the disastrous results of the Renegade album and Phil's latest's solo dud, Lizzy's management team debated on how to save the franchise from total bankruptcy.

It was decided that Lizzy would be going on a farewell tour in 1983 and after that Lizzy would be buried forever. Phil was sick at the thought of saying good-bye to his real family but went about it cool and collected. It's generally believed that he never wanted to end Lizzy but by this point in their careers, all involved except for the youngsters Sykes and Wharton (unfortunate timing for them) needed a break from the Thin Lizzy express.

With the announcement of a final Thin Lizzy farewell tour tickets were snatched up at once. With one foot in their rock n' roll graves they hit the road for the musical equivalent of an Irish wake. By the time March came around Thunder and Lightning catapulted to #4 on the album charts heralding that Thin Lizzy was going out in a blaze of glory. Sykes provided the ingredients that had been missing since Gary Moore's inspired shredding on the Black Rose album and everyone from the members of Lizzy, to the press and most importantly the fans knew it as they watched the live broadcast from the Regal Theatre in Hitchin, on the BBC's Sight and Sound in Concert program series. Sykes brought fire-breathing heavy metal playing to a whole new audience and Phil proved again what an excellent front man he was despite his bloated and distant appearance. Especially in how he continued to control the crowd with ease, even cracking a hilarious joke as he introduced "The Boys are back in Town" as a "Medley of our hit" bringing a ripple of laughter out of the crowd.

In February the single "Cold Sweat" was released and hit #27 on the charts but Phil's stoned encounter and later argument with a Top of the Pops producer nixed their scheduled performance on the show and ultimately helped sink the single which slipped down and out of the charts a few weeks later. The song was super heavy and full of great story telling that could have provided the band with another MTV worthy video but once again the record company dropped the ball. The album sold well upon its release on March 4th, 1983 and was a good sign that Lizzy the rockers had returned to form. It's a shame that the Thunder and Lightning album and tour would be the last to feature John Sykes, because it's apparent upon hearing that if Phil and Scott had managed to kick the drugs and stay sober Lizzy's new lineup could have contributed greatly to the metal ruling decade of the 1980's. Thunder and Lightning opens with a burst of thunder echoes and the guitar smoking style of John Sykes. The inspired title track makes its intentions clear that this was going to be an album that pussies should avoid if they valued their eardrums. Brian's drumming is awoken from its slumber and he gets co-writing credit on a monster of a way to kick off a new album. It makes you want to smash someone's face in and takes us back to when Lizzy was known as a gang that you didn't want to meet in a dark alley at three in the morning. "Thunder and Lightning" is metal as it gets and peaked at #39 on the singles charts in May. Phil's songwriting spectacularly returns to form and despite the abused vocal chords he sings with a convicted warning that says don't make me fuck you up. It's teen angst at its finest.

The hard rocking metal madness continues with the solid second track "This is the One" a tune co-written by Darren Wharton and full of wonderful musical moments. Brian's drums are fast and neck snapping and the riffs Sykes came up with add the metal touch especially during the chorus, which is beautifully song by Phil. It's like a riot at the steel factory and Sykes scorches his solo…

I've got to find an occupation, I've got to keep myself employed

It's a bad situation, my brains destroyed, destroyed

I've got to find a new vocation, I feel it burning down inside

Such a low down abrasion, inside it hurts my pride

I hear it, I know it, I touch it, I feel it, I see it

Some day we will have won, I can feel it in my bones

This is the one

Phil and Wharton team up again on the albums third track, the hauntingly beautiful ballad "The Sun Goes Down". Released as Thin Lizzy's final single it stalled at # 52 on Aug. 6, 1983 and sailed into obscurity shortly after. Listening to it thirty years later it's a stunning testament to how great Thin Lizzy and Phil Lynott were as musicians, songwriters, and overall artists. The track is intensely structured and the solos from Sykes and Scott are blistering while the chord changes and bridges remained subdued. Wharton's synth work and pad layering is phenomenal and Phil sings like a dying man making one last confession before he turns his soul over Satan. It's the slowest song on Thunder and Lightning, a stunning yet simple ode to the eternal struggle of good vs. evil. A battle that Phil was starting to realize he might be losing. The pace picks up with the funk metal number "The Holy War" a track about religion that Phil tackles like an old school Chicago Bears linebacker. Phil was battling a lot of inner demons and the "Sun Goes Down" and "Holy War" are both prime examples that indeed the poet from days yore was still inside him. The middle of the album features Thin Lizzy's last charting semi-hit "Cold Sweat", with its theme of a vagabond gambler, the song was a natural to be filmed in Las Vegas where the maximum effect of a great music video could have been achieved. However this idea remains only in a Lizzy fans dreams as the record company shot no video for the track and did no real promotion thus sealing its fate. Phil seems to use the Valentino character from "Waiting For An Alibi" and some feel that the song is a much better and focused if not heavier sequel to the Black Rose classic. Tracks number six "Someday she is going to hit Back" a tune about domestic violence and number seven "Baby please don't Go" are back-to-back fillers that kill the albums stunning metal momentum. Track number eight is the hypnotic "Bad Habits" the final great Lynott-Gorham collaboration. The chorus is perfect and Scott brings back some of his early pre-junk Lizzy magic to the guitar parts. Phil's lyrics feel like they were inspired by a Woody Allen movie. The final Thin Lizzy song "Heart Attack" is fittingly another Lynott-Gorham collaboration that has Phil pouring his heart out one last time. The man seems to know that it's all going to shit…

Mama I'm dying of a heart attack, heart attack, heart attack

I love that girl but she don't love me back

My girl she tells me that we're breaking up, breaking up, breaking up

My heart can't handle the strain that's shaking it

She tried to tell me no so long ago

I would not listen but now I know

Papa I'm drinking for an overload, overload, overload

The gun in my pocket is all ready to explode

The album's cover that some consider corny and Fitzpatrick claimed was done on the cheap to avoid paying him for another original art piece has become another Lizzy conundrum. Although some feel the cover was too Spinal Tap like to be taken serious, the image of a black leather glove sticking out of the ground with a guitar in the background being struck by lightning has become iconic heavy metal imagery. In high spirits during a photo shoot for the album Phil joked about the album cover to Kerrang!:

This is the first time we've had an album ready that's coming out on schedule for the tour and we're stuck for an idea for the cover. It's proving to be much harder than we thought. I mean check out how many groups have used a lightning bolt either on their sleeves or as a logo. Dire Straits and AC/DC being two classic examples. Jeez isn't it fookin' typical it's as if we're fated to bring out our albums no matter what, I mean if we had everything ready I bet something would go wrong, something like the pressing plant would blow up, hargh, hargh.[46]

Thin Lizzy's farewell tour culminated in an epic show at the Hammersmith that featured ex-Lizzy guitarists Robbo, Bell, and Moore on stage together playing "The Rocker" in an all-star jam. These recordings and others from the farewell tour surfaced on Lizzy's final contractually obligated album Life, a live album that was mixed lazily muddied and sorely missed the magic touch of Tony Visconti. It charted at #29 upon its release in the fall of 1983 and remains interesting because it features the only official live shredding from Sykes as a member of Thin Lizzy.

To Scott the farewell tour seemed to go on forever and after a bad spell in Japan where he and Phil failed to score heroin, the enthusiasm and energy required to give a shit about performing anymore completely evaporated. The last stand for Lizzy was on September 4th, 1983 at the Monsters of Rock festival in Nuremberg, Germany. After this show the band members flew back to Heathrow airport in London, gathered their bags and waved goodbye to each other as they all went their separate ways. The unceremonious end to rock's most underappreciated band.

None actually believed that Lizzy wouldn't get back together again and felt that they just needed a break. Especially Scott who was concerned if he didn't get help immediately with his drug addiction he wouldn't live much longer. He hoped that Phil would do the same but unfortunately the poet rocker didn't have the same intestinal fortitude. The closing chapter of Thin Lizzy's historic fifteen-year ride came to an anti-climactic end at Heathrow as the boys walked out of the airport and into the history books as another tragic tale of rock. Following Thin Lizzy's demise Philip's heroin use continued to worsen and his wife Caroline now seeing the writing on the wall threatened to leave him. She finally did near the end of 1983, taking their children back to Bath in the hope this would finally shake Lynott out of his complacent drug slumber. But now facing a broken marriage, a defunct band, and debilitating drug addiction, Lynott slipped further into oblivion. Confronted with the reality of losing both of his families, Phil pondered where it all went wrong while chasing the dragon in some seedy and lonely London hotel room. As 1984 loomed, the sun began to fade on Phil's life and the luck of the Irish abandoned him.

The Sun goes Down

Nor dread nor hope attend

A dying animal; A man awaits his end

Dreading and hoping all; Many times he died

Many times rose again

A great man in his pride

Confronting murderous men

Casts derision upon Supersession of breath

He knows death to the bone

Man has created death

W.B. Yeats

For Phil, the disintegration of Thin Lizzy and the sudden separation of his wife and kids was the beginning of the end. Not that Phil was 100% faithful to Caroline anyways, like most rock stars he had trouble keeping his dick in his pants when not at home. Without his family or his band Phil sank deep into depression, took his heroin intake to new levels and grew apart from everyone. He refused help and didn't believe his drug abuse that was that much of a big deal. Although at the time Phil never truly believed that Thin Lizzy's last stand would be that gig in Nuremberg, secretly it was killing him to accept that Lizzy had been a failure. Thin Lizzy held a much deeper meaning to Phil than to every other musician that came through its ranks and he had spent more time with his musical brethren (Thin Lizzy) then with his actual real family. He was the wild rover, vagabond, and Irish trailblazer that he sung and wrote about but as 1984 dragged on, Phil found himself alone, strung out and isolated for the first time in his life. The walks along Burrow beach with Jim Fitzpatrick no longer contained enthusiastic chatter and the days of playing soccer amongst the Irish sands with the boys had long ceased to exist.

Instead of seeking help and resting Phil put together another band and hit the Showband circuit in a failed attempt at recapturing his youth. Grand Slam was put together post-Lizzy and was pretty much doomed from the start. It took ages for Phil to even come up with a name for the band and soon after it formed, drummer Brian Downey quit the project claiming that he didn't see the point in making a half-ass version of Thin Lizzy. Guitarist John Sykes walked out on Phil after accepting an offer from David Coverdale to join Whitesnake. An old friend from his Dublin Skid Row days, Robbie Brennan replaced Brian on Drums and Laurence Archer took over on lead guitar. The group had a second guitarist and also a keyboard player similar to the setup of the late Lizzy. When Slam toured throughout the rest of 1984, critics and fans responded negatively to this perceived low-grade version of Thin Lizzy. Some decent songs arose from the demo sessions that were primarily recorded in Lynott's Richmond home recording studio and a week-long session at Lombard's in Dublin. Despite the media backlash Phil was committed to Grand Slam and rehearsed vigorously before an important gig at the London Marquee. Prior to the show he told a reporter from Kerrang! "I'm really fighting for Grand Slam at the moment. I mean, we're here rehearsing 6 days a week, from two in the afternoon until ten at night. I'm really pushing a heavy emphasis on my playing and it's standing me in good stead because it has improved. When it comes down to it though I do feel that the future of the band lies in America. If we head over there and work on it for a time then we can come back to England and not have to face the usual crap that gets flung in my direction I'm not fashionable here anymore so once we complete this tour that should be our next move." Phil was deeply troubled at failing to cross over into America especially after having such a huge hit with "The Boys" and the realization of never being able to recapture that moment in time crushed him.

Making it worse was the fact that the bridge he helped build for musicians to cross over from Ireland was being used to stunning success by the rock group Def Leopard. A band that in 1984 sold seven millions records in America and was kept from having a #1 record on the billboard charts only because they were competing with Michael Jackson's Thriller. Phil offered excuses to Lizzy's failed conquering of America, claiming that the percentage points that they would have to give up to tour and promote extensively in America didn't make sense considering that they were selling huge amounts of records in Europe and the UK and for a band just starting out it would be in Def Leopard's favor to give those points away. Even though what Phil says is true it's still a pretty poor excuse considering that the fault of never having made it in America was Lizzy's just as it was their record company's ineptness. After a blistering set at the Marquee Phil's hopes improved about a landing a record deal but the suits seemed uninterested on signing a known drug addict destroying his legacy during a mid-life crisis. Ultimately Grand Slam like its inventor was doomed but listening to the remastered demos released in 2002, there's a fair share of quality material composed by them. Although the songs were more New Wave than rock n' roll, Phil's songwriting capabilities were still prevalent despite being weighed down by an unwavering heroin addiction. One example is the spectacular song "The Sisters of Mercy" a tune that had a new wave vibe full of outstanding lyrics, riffs, and keyboard melodies. "Harlem" was another lyrical gem that Phil wrote in 1984, and the track has a funky Hip-Hop feel to it. The remaining Grand Slam recordings are more musical than lyrical but the sessions did provide Phil with some last minute songwriting glory in the form of a Gary Moore single and B-side.

For Phil, the end of the Grand Slam experiment occurred during the summer of 1985 when he ventured to California to shoot a music video. When he returned he learned that the members of Slam had abandoned the group to pursue other musical paths. Phil was essentially dumped but almost immediately after his fortunes improved with the offer of another solo album deal and a possible publication of his short stories. Before the break up of Slam Phil wrote and sang on Clann Eadair's tribute single to the late Sandy Denny and produced and appeared in Auto Da Fe's video "Man of Mine". But Phil's reputation had suffered greatly within the higher echelon of music circles and his Manager Chris Morrison quit producing Grand Slam after sinking $100,000 dollars of his own money on the ill-fated experiment. With no money to support the band Grand Slam finally ended in 1985 and Phil's bloated and heavy appearance began to send shockwaves throughout the industry.

Tony Clayton-Lea interviewed Phil for Hot Press in 1984:

Tony Clayton-Lea: I know it's been recounted before, Philip, but what thoughts do you have now on the demise of Thin Lizzy?

Philip Lynott: I was sorry to see it go... everybody thought it was a scam, that we'd be back together again in six months. Maybe it's because I'm such a proficient liar... but there was no way around it, it was definitely goin' to end. And now it's gone, it's never goin' to come back. It's like your virginity... that's the way I feel. It was a good band, I was very pleased to be in it...I thought 18 months ago I'd learnt lessons in humility... I mean, you do get used to people runnin' around after you, carryin' your guitar case, doin' this, that, and the other. When it's done constantly, you start to take it for granted. You start expecting the amps to be ready when you walk in to play, the equipment to be set up. Obviously, I'll still expect that in certain situations. For rehearsals, I don't mind settin' everythin' up. I do mind if I'm payin' somebody to do it, like in the Lizzy situation. Because people treat you as important, you begin to think that maybe you're a little bit more important than you are. You always have to look in the mirror, though. It never got out of hand.

Tony Clayton-Lea: Is Philip Lynott a religious person?

Philip Lynott: As I get older I get more religious... because I'm goin' to die fookin' soon. The odds are more in God's favor. I'd say it's almost like bein' Irish and Catholic. Once you're Irish and Catholic, you're always Irish and Catholic. I think it's in you. You can never disassociate yourself from it. You can acquire another accent, but it'll always be there in your head. The rules that were beaten into me at school are ingrained.

Tony Clayton-Lea: Were you ever verbally or physically abused because of your color?

Philip Lynott: Er... you mean attacked? A couple of times people have said something, but we buried them shortly afterwards.

Tony Clayton-Lea: What's your favorite drug?

Philip Lynott: Sugar... I'm off the ciggies... Alcohol, it must be. I'm not a lush, but I do like a drink sometimes...I think drugs are there to be used. If you're goin' to ask me about drugs in general, as opposed to 'drug' drugs... that's the reason why I mentioned sugar and alcohol; to show that there are a lot of drugs about that you aren't even aware of. I found out that tomato ketchup has 23% sugar in it. I've got this big thing against sugar at the moment, 'cos I'm the father of kids... all those Easter eggs...'Drug' drugs are really bad for you. They can cause you an awful lot of misery. Initially, you get some great kicks, and it does give you different perspectives, and you can find all the reasons in the world for taking them, but there's just as many reasons for not taking them. In fact, more. The reasons for not taking them obviously include addiction, they can change your personality without you knowin', so you lose control of your mind and body, and therefore you lose your dignity. And the stigma attached to taking drugs socially is bad news. A lot of people look to Keith Richards, and hold him in reverence, like a hero, but I know if Keith had his life again - he said to me - he wouldn't do them again. Sid Vicious is also held in reverence. He was just a guy fucked up on dope. It sounds like you're preachin' or condescending', like (adopts admonitory accent) 'Don't take drugs, I've been there'. So I'm not even goin' to try. Just don't. If anybody really wants to find out about drugs, they should go to a Narcotics Anonymous meeting.

Tony Clayton-Lea: What do you think of the present heroin situation in Dublin?

Philip Lynott: It's bad, it really is...I'd like to know more about the situation before I could give you a positive reply. At the moment, I can't see a solution to it. For the past 15 years you've been living a lifestyle that condones - sometimes encourages - the easy availability of drugs and sex. I don't agree with that. I think the media picked up on those aspects, and blew them up out of proportion. I remember there was a film out, called 'The Stud', starring Oliver Tobias. Me and Oliver were knockin' about at the time, and he was stuck in one room, and I was in another doing an interview with the Daily Mirror and I had a studded leather bracelet on. Anyway next day, I buy the paper, and it's like 'The Black Stud'. I do things that are wrong. I make mistakes like everybody else as far as society is concerned. I don't try and promote that. If you listen carefully to all those songs, 'Got To Give It Up' or 'The Opium Trail', which is actually - jokin' aside - an anti-drug song. The message is fairly serious. Now, to speak about such things, you have to be experienced - Have you ever been experienced? Well, I have.' Some of the things I'm proud of. Some of the things I'm not. I'd hate to think that I encouraged people to go over the rails, y'know what I mean? I always thought that I was sharin', laughin' with the people. I'd hate to think I was corruptin' them. [47]

Long time Phil Lynott supporter, Irish musical hero and former Thin Lizzy road manager Frank Murray reflected on Phil's last days to Hot Press in 2011:

Phil was a very complex man, again because of his generation. We used to go watch Elvis in his early movies and the characters he played were kind of tough no-nonsense people. Phil often used to quote that thing from Kid Creole, 'I ain't no grease monkey. I ain't gonna slide for you'. Skid Row toured America twice and Gary Moore was this great guitar player and Brush was a great bass player and Noel Bridgman was an incredible drummer, but the one thing that Philip had over any of those people was that he was a star…The attitude to drugs in the early days was far more lax than it is now. Back then it was regarded as a bit of a weird thing to do, but you were less likely to be hassled about it by the cops or customs staff. For example, I remember a bunch of us smoking joints on a plane and the stewardess just laughed at us. Then the big stuff came in and Ireland was flooded with cocaine and heroin and gradually it became harder and harder to be seen to use any kind of drugs at all. When the criminal gangs got involved something had to be done about it. When Phil came back to Dublin, the doors had just opened on the heroin rush. Heroin was available to every single body. And when Lizzy finished and he tried to put together Grand Slam he was too far gone to create it. I think his creative muse was hibernating somewhere. Put it this way, had he given up Thin Lizzy earlier, and had he been confident about recording a solo album, staying at home, kicking back for a year, playing around in the home studio, doing the things that you're supposed to do, that are kind of normal, I think his songwriting would have developed in a different way. He would have really delivered. He still had so much to give when he died.[48]

For Phil, 1984 had been a year devoted to a drug habit that finally begun to overrun his life. His marriage was over, and unable to clean up his appearance left Phil without visitation privileges to his two daughters Sarah and Cathleen. Many people tried to speak with him, but unfortunately he failed to acknowledge or even realize his predicament. Phil did still have some fight left in him and it only took the resolve of longtime friend and ex-Lizzy member Gary Moore to bring it stunningly back out of him. In 1985, Moore rescued his old buddy and placed him back in the top ten on the charts for the last time. Phil was already in good songwriting form having spent the first half of 1985 working with Huey Lewis and the UK R&B sensation Junior. These tracks have been leaked in various bootleg editions and despite the jagged sound quality they remain interesting anecdotes to Phil's unique musical catalogue.

Phil's duet with Junior "The Lady loves to Dance" is an excellent song that could have been a hit single in the vein of 80's style R&B like you would hear from Billy Ocean. The song was even submitted as a single by Junior but Phil's record company blocked its release and to this day Phil's versatility in being able to work with R&B star Junior outside the rock element has never had a proper release. Another lost song from 1985 was "Freedom comes" a track that rocks but it's the fantastic bass work and social commentary found in "Hard Times" that proved Phil had plenty of street poet left inside him…

Hard times

There are people in the bread line

Bad days

There are people that say she is a saint

Nobody prays

Hey mister I made a mistake

I have taken all the love I can take

In this time it's getting rough

Hard Times

There are people on the streets dying

Such bad breaks

My heart aches

My body shakes

I have taken all the love I can take

You wait till you see what happens next

They won't complain

Just throw a bomb

You try and you try

Now they won't leave you alone

They turn your heart to stone

You cry and you cry

Love they won't leave me alone

Hard times

Nobody waits

Phil's last great ballad "Samantha" an excellent collaboration with John Sykes was recorded at his home studio during the early months of 1985, but it was his reteaming with Gary Moore that gave Phil his last shot at the big time. Gary had a new album slated for release and needed a single to promote it. He had arranged the anti-war track "Out in the fields" and sought Phil's lyrical prowess to make the track work. Phil quickly obliged and keeping the anti-war theme going decided to rework a Grand Slam cut "Military Man" with Gary as the B-side. It was a masterstroke of luminosity and shocked everyone when the record shot to #5 on the singles charts. "Out in the fields" is a great tale about the horrors of war that Phil turns into a personal plea to his mother and daughters. "Out in the Fields" is unquestionably one of the greatest anti-war songs ever written and Phil's final lyrical jewel…

It doesn't matter

If you're wrong or if you're right

It makes no difference

If you're black or if you're white

All men are equal

Till the victory is won

No color or religion

Ever stopped the bullet from a gun

The video showing Gary and Phil dressed in Military uniforms intercut with shots of Belfast street violence had a huge impact on the songs relevance. Its stunning social commentary and unexpected chart bombing became a staple of discussion amongst early morning British television and the hardcore video a fixture of late night music video programs. Phil and Gary were back on prime time getting excellent exposure with awesome performances on the Old Grey Whistle Test, The Saturday Picture Show, and Razzamatazz. But it was their botched performance on ECT that has remained a low point in television broadcast history. The ECT cut off Phil and Gary during the introduction of "Still in love with you" thus robbing the television audience of witnessing one of Gary Moore's greatest solos. When Gary discovered this travesty he became sick as hell and hunted down the terrified producers of the show threatening to kick all of their asses.

Phil was back on the charts and Polydor offered him a deal for his third solo album to be released in 1986. The success of "Out in the Fields" also shot Gary Moore into the mainstream and his album Run for Cover, which featured the hit single, became the first of four consecutive gold albums for Moore. Gary would pen an epic tribute song "Blood of Emeralds" in honor of Phil a few years after his Irish homeboy's untimely death. Gary's lyrics are autobiographical and powerfully sung…

I was born up on the North side

Where the Lagan River flows

When I came across the border

I was following my nose

Dublin city '69

There could have been no better place

There was no better time

Through the thunder and the rain

The deepest blood of emeralds

Was running through my veins

I was down and out on Skid Row

But I held on to my pride

The darkest son of Ireland

He was standin' by my side

We would sail the stormy seas

Never looking back

We were afraid of what we'd see

Through the thunder and the rain

The deepest blood of emeralds

Was running through our veins

By the summer of 1985 things had picked up for Phil and with the talk of the upcoming Live Aid charity concert rumors began swirling that Thin Lizzy were getting back together to perform at the epic event. Organized by Midge Ure and Bob Geldof, two of Phil's friends and people that he helped put on the map musically, the event was staged as a massive one-off globally broadcast concert to help out the famine situation in Ethiopia. The concert has since become iconic and was responsible for launching the career of U2, another band that benefitted greatly from the bridge across Ireland Phil helped to establish. Queen gave one of their best performances at Live Aid and it's sad to say that Thin Lizzy was never even asked to perform. Geldof nor Ure even bothered to ask Phil if he wanted to rock Live Aid and although rumors had buzzed for weeks at a possible Thin Lizzy reunion none of the boys were asked to rock. Geldof at first said that Phil wasn't that big anymore and then backtracked years later to wondering why they never asked Thin Lizzy to perform at Live Aid to even going as far as claiming that he wished Phil was still alive because he would be a king.

It's been speculated that Phil's declining health and continual drug use made him unreliable, but he was fit enough to jam with Gary Moore and had he been asked, like a true friend would have, there's no doubt that Phil could have cleaned up and put the proper focus into reuniting Thin Lizzy for a one-off performance that would have knocked their socks off. Phil was sick at not being invited to perform at Live Aid and no doubt must have been severely depressed after watching Freddie Mercury completely own 72,000 screaming fans at Wembley Stadium knowing that he was never given the same chance. Live Aid was a massive success and one of the largest satellite and television broadcasts of all time, spanning over 150 countries and being seen by an estimated two billion people. It also made Ure and Geldof extremely rich as Live Aid grossed more than 283 million dollars. It's never been clear just how much money actually went to Ethiopia but rest assured it wasn't 200 million dollars. Geldof was now a media mogul and obtained an honorary knighthood from Queen Elizabeth and was even awarded a Nobel Peace prize. But to Thin Lizzy fans he remains an asshole of the highest order. He's also considered an asshole to the fans of INXS, who claim that Geldof had lead singer Michael Hutchence killed after the INXS hunk stole Bob's wife Paula Yates in 1995. According to Paula's police statement given on the day of Hutchence's death, Geldof believed he was "Above the law" thanks to his riches and the higher occult circles of the British elite he moved in after the success of Live Aid. These same circles would later lay claim to his daughter Peaches who some believed was sacrificed for exposing the secrets of the illuminati.

However not everyone was fooled by Geldof and Ure's scheme, iconic American rocker and the eternally cool Frank Zappa claimed to Howard Stern in 1985 that, "Live Aid was the biggest cocaine money laundering scheme of all time." For Phil not being invited to play Live Aid and essentially getting dissed by two guys that were supposed to be his friends drove the final stake through his already fragile heart. Darren Wharton recalled Phil's and ultimately Thin Lizzy's exclusion from Live Aid as, "a tragic, tragic decision. This could've been a turning point for Phil, who at the time had some substance problems. It could've been and it should've been the turning point for Phil. And I think that really did Phil in quite a lot, that we were never asked to play. I mean Phil, had a few problems at the time, but at the end of the day, if he would've been asked to play Live Aid, that would've been a goal for him to clean himself up to do that gig. We were all very upset of the fact that we weren't asked to do it. Because as you say, it was Geldof and Midge who Phil knew very well. I was surprised that we weren't asked to do that. That would've been the turning point, you know, definitely. I don't think Phil ever forgave Bob and Midge for that really."

Despite the bad shape he was in, Midge and Geldof practically owed him at least an invitation considering how much Phil had not only done for them but all other Irish musicians. A bloated and sweaty Phil dropped by Ireland's RTE studios during the broadcast and dipped out an hour later disgusted at being rejected. That evening he disappeared into some black tar heroin and days later a disenfranchised Lynott talked with Jim Fitzpatrick about the heartache that being left out of Live Aid had caused him. Fitzpatrick recalled, "That was a cruel day. I believe Live Aid destroyed him because he was Ireland's biggest rock star and he was excluded. Maybe he couldn't do it. Maybe he was so far gone. I'm condemning no one. But the fact he didn't appear on Live Aid had a huge amount to do with him going downhill. I know that because he told me." As the summer of 1985 progressed Phil attended Gary Moore's wedding in Lincolnshire and booked time to record at Polydor's London studio.

Phil began working on his hopeful third solo album but couldn't kick the drug habit, and everyone from Robbo to Jerome Rimson begged him to clean up his act if he valued his music and his family. Their pleas fell on deaf ears and even Phil's planned family vacation to Marbella, Spain resulted in more boozing and junking. Phil flew a few members of Grand Slam to Spain to help him with a solo show, but the gig was a disaster and after a botched 4 a.m. performance of the "Boys are back" the concert was over and the band went back to boozing it up. Phil returned alone to his Glenn Corr estate in Ireland and feeling tapped out creatively, holed himself up avoiding any contact with the outside world. One person that was able to gain access was Phil's longtime friend Smiley Bolger, but Smiley soon found himself literally thrown out the front door landing on his ass after he confronted Phil about his crippling drug habit.

By September Phil had returned to London and acquired the red-hot producer Paul Hardcastle to help produce what ultimately became Phil's last official single "Nineteen". Hardcastle was one of the pioneers of electronic music and already had a #1 hit ironically titled "19" when he and Phil joined forces. Phil was eager to take chances and loved the idea of expanding his sound into dance music territory knowing that Hardcastle was one of the genre's trailblazers. Phil even managed to borrow a motorcycle and brought it inside the studio for Hardcastle to record the revving of the pipes. Phil spent about ten minutes smoking out the studio and had a good laugh at the chaos the stunt caused. Phil was more driven than ever and pushed Hardcastle for a disco sound that throbbed on the dance floor but still fucking rocked. When Phil couldn't figure out a decent bassline he walked off for a smoke, leaving his bass on the studio floor. Hardcastle picked up Phil's bass and began experimenting with some riffs; he eventually recorded a few of them and nervously played them to Phil upon his arrival back at the studio. Phil was impressed and Hardcastle's basslines were used in the final mix of the song. They spent an additional two weeks mastering the track and once it was decided that "Nineteen" would be the lead single off Phil's third solo album they met at Phil's Kew Road home for a photo shoot. Hardcastle was impressed by Phil's jukebox and a charitable Phil gave it to Hardcastle a few weeks later as a late wedding gift. Phil even sent letters to Paul's new wife with a note apologizing for keeping her husband out working so late.

In October, Phil flew to California to record the video for "Nineteen" a song that was inspired by a Biker Phil met at a bar in Texas. The biker had a bunch of tattoos and belonged to the 19th chapter of the Hells Angels. While in California Phil shot the video on Halloween night and hired a bunch of real Hells Angels bikers to appear in the video. While Phil wasn't physically in the best mood for the video shoot, thanks to partying in Hollywood the previous evening with actors Richard Gere and Matt Dillon, the assembled mix of bikers and the bass player from Twisted Sister all made up for a rousing music video shoot that stretched from the California deserts to the astonished gazes of the folks found on Hollywood Blvd.

In late November, and only a month away from meeting the reaper Phil began working with members of Huey Lewis and his band The News in a studio in foggy San Francisco. The tracks Phil recorded with Huey Lewis while hanging out in Frisco are more great examples of just how good Phil could be when branching out. He didn't need to always be the rocker, he could just about pull off any other style that he wanted to with ease. The only thing that really stood in his way was the heroin monster. The three tracks Phil composed with Huey Lewis in San Francisco "Can't get Away" "Still Alive" and "One Wish" are stunning pop songs that have that perfect 80's musical vibe to them. It's no doubt they would have been featured on Phil's third solo album and released around the same time that Huey Lewis began to blow up in America. Phil sadly died right before Huey's fame exploded with the release of the #1 song "Power of Love" featured in the blockbuster film Back to the Future. Huey skyrocketed to fame and fortune becoming an iconic pop figure in the annals of American rock history and there's no doubt that the man that taught Huey everything he knew would have been right there enjoying the ride.

Phil's final recordings were done in December. "Do you want to Rock?" was done with Colbert Hamilton three weeks before his death. Phil played bass and sung backup vocals on a track that sat underneath Hamilton's bed for nearly twenty-five years. Phil's last known recordings were the crunching anti-government songs "No More" and "Revolution" done with guitarist Steve Johnson, tracks that even in their rough demo states proved that Phil still had plenty of music left in the tank. However the fates had other plans and when Phil's single "Nineteen" was released it hit the pop charts with little fanfare reaching no higher than #76 and soon dropped out of sight completely. Phil made his last appearance on television with a cracking live performance complete with motorcycles on the Razzamatazz Christmas Special.

But despite the push to get Lynott's solo career reignited the bad rep he earned as a member of Thin Lizzy and the anti-drug mood that all of England was wrapped up in ultimately sealed the single's fate. The failure of "Nineteen" finally did him in and as the holidays approached Phil holed himself up at his Kew Road home in Richmond. Brian joined Phil to discuss the possibility of putting Thin Lizzy back together but refused to do anything until Phil kicked his drug habit. Brian left back to Ireland the next morning and the drum n' bass partners since fourteen years old would never speak to each other again. A clean and sobered up Scott visited and couldn't believe how bad a shape Phil was in. Scott recalled his heartbreaking final visit with his best friend, "I knew when he answered the door he was still in a bad way. He had put on weight, his breathing was heavy, and though he spoke positively about the future I just thought it would take a little time before he got back on form again. So we kicked around a few ideas, had a chat basically and wished each other a good Christmas and said that we'd meet up soon." Like Brian, Scott's final encounter with Phil was at the doomed rocker's Kew Road estate. After Phil assured him that he would be "going on the big clean and cutting the shit out" Scott would never again have the chance of seeing Phil alive.

As Christmas approached Santa Claus wasn't the only one hovering above Phil's home. The black cloud of death was nearby, and the grim reaper revved up his Harley getting ready to descend below and claim one of his own.

Redemption

Believe me, if all those endearing young charms

Which I gaze on so fondly to-day

Were to change by to-morrow, and fleet in my arms

Live fairy-gifts fading away

Thou wouldst still be adored, as this moment thou art

Let thy loveliness fade as it will

And around the dear ruin each wish of my heart

Would entwine itself verdantly still

It is not while beauty and youth are thine own

And thy cheeks unprofaned by a tear

That the fervor and faith of a soul may be known

To which time will but make thee more dear!

No, the heart that has truly loved never forgets

But as truly loves on to the close

As the sunflower turns on her god when he sets

The same look which she turned when he rose!

Thomas Moore

Christmas for the Lynott family was just like Christmas for all other families with the only exception being a little holiday smack to compliment your rum soaked eggnog. Phil had tried to score prior to Christmas Eve, but his plans were thwarted by the appearance of roadie Charlie McClellan. Charlie laid it straight to Phil's mother after seeing the devastating state that Phil was in. Up until this moment Philomena never knew just how bad Phil's heroin addiction was. He always lied to her when she asked him if he was taking hard drugs. Hard drugs of course were of the opiate variety. Previous to 9/11 the Taliban had managed to eliminate over half of the world's opium supply. But as of 2015 that same supply rose by 75% after the invasion and overthrow by American and British forces in Afghanistan. With the popularity of synthetics pills like OxyContin, and an estimated global yearly profit of more than 70 billion dollars, hard drugs have flooded society now more than ever, and were still easily available to Phil during the holidays of 1985. That is until Charlie showed up and slammed Phil up against the wall of his own house.

Phil denied the accusations that Charlie hurled at Philomena and after twenty minutes of screaming and name-calling Charlie left the house mad as hell. But Philomena took another good look at Phil and for the first time began to see him in an un-angelic light. She noticed the bloated features, and the puffiness of Phil's face, sort of like how her teenage screen idol Errol Flynn's looked during his last days. She knew at that moment that Phil was sick and time slowed down to her as she looked for solace in the kitchen. The hours after Charlie left were relatively quiet until Phil's pusher tried to leave something for him in the mailbox. Philomena just happened to catch him and ran after the bloke kicking and punching and screaming at the smack dealer. She was furious as Phil stepped outside and watched his dealer scramble off into the distance. She now had the proof in her hands and a teary eyed Phil could no longer lie to his mom.

Without the aid of smack in his system Phil's ravished body began to go into withdrawals. He fought it long enough to open some Christmas presents with his two daughters. They were happy and all smiles for a brief moment before Phil suddenly collapsed. Philomena became hysterical and put Phil in a cold bath to help him recover. It worked just long enough to get him conscious and by the time Phil's estranged wife Caroline showed up, it was decided that she would drive him to the nearest rehab center. But the only place open on Christmas day was two hours away in Salisbury. Caroline drove Phil to the center and lord knows what was going on in her mind as the father of her two girls was knocking on heaven's gate, spread out in the backseat behind her. After the doctors at the rehab center saw the dire situation Phil was in they quickly sent him to the hospital's infirmary in downtown Salisbury.

Phil languished between sleeping and being conscious long enough to have brief conversations with his mother. Philomena stayed by her son's side the whole time, as Phil's body slowly broke down. His liver, kidneys and heart were failing due to the years of hard living and the alcohol, cigarettes and junk destroyed whatever was left of his inner organs. Rock n' roll excess was about to kill Phil and his last wish was to call in a priest for a private conversation concerning god and the next realm. Naturally Philomena was the last to speak to Phil and she cries every time she recalls his last words. With tears in his eyes, Phil apologized to his mother and said with his dying breath "Merciful Jesus what have I done to you." After Phil had passed on due to sepsis and heart failure from pneumonia, Philomena gasped as she got a good look at the tracks in Phil's feet and ankles. That's where he shot up and how he was able to deceive everyone. Here's a man that rose from crippling poverty and was able to buy houses for not only his mother but also himself and his wife, but couldn't kick the one habit that can instantly make all your material possessions, riches and talent null and void. His body deteriorating to the point of comatose Phil lingered unresponsively for eleven days before his spirit slipped away.

It was a devastating blow to Philomena and Phil's family. He had been sick before and had an amazing resolve so the thought that Phil, an Irish superhero could actually die was unheard of. When Brian and Scott found out that he was in the hospital they didn't bother going because they figured he would get well soon like he always had done. But not this time, Phil the rocker had finally joined his leather-clad heroes in the afterlife. The sudden announcement of his death sent shockwaves throughout the music industry and the world at large. Brian heard the news on the radio and Scott received a phone call that crushingly sent him to weep alone on the edge of the stairs. Jim Fitzpatrick wrote about the day Phil died on his website:

For some reason I always thought that Philip was immortal. If we got drenched in the same rain storm, he'd sit there in his wet clothes, smoking a joint, while I would have my clothes out on the rads and my hair under a dryer. Still, I'd end up sniffling for a week while he'd be out partying every night. And so I reacted with complete and utter incredulity to the news of his death. Ironically it was in the Bailey, his favorite haunt, that I first heard of his death. I had been out all day and missed the phone calls and I was having a lunch hour drink with my ex-wife and two old friends of Philips', Tony Higgins and Tom Collins, when a guy opposite lifted up his early edition evening newspaper and we read the headline 'PHILIP LYNOTT DEAD'.[45]

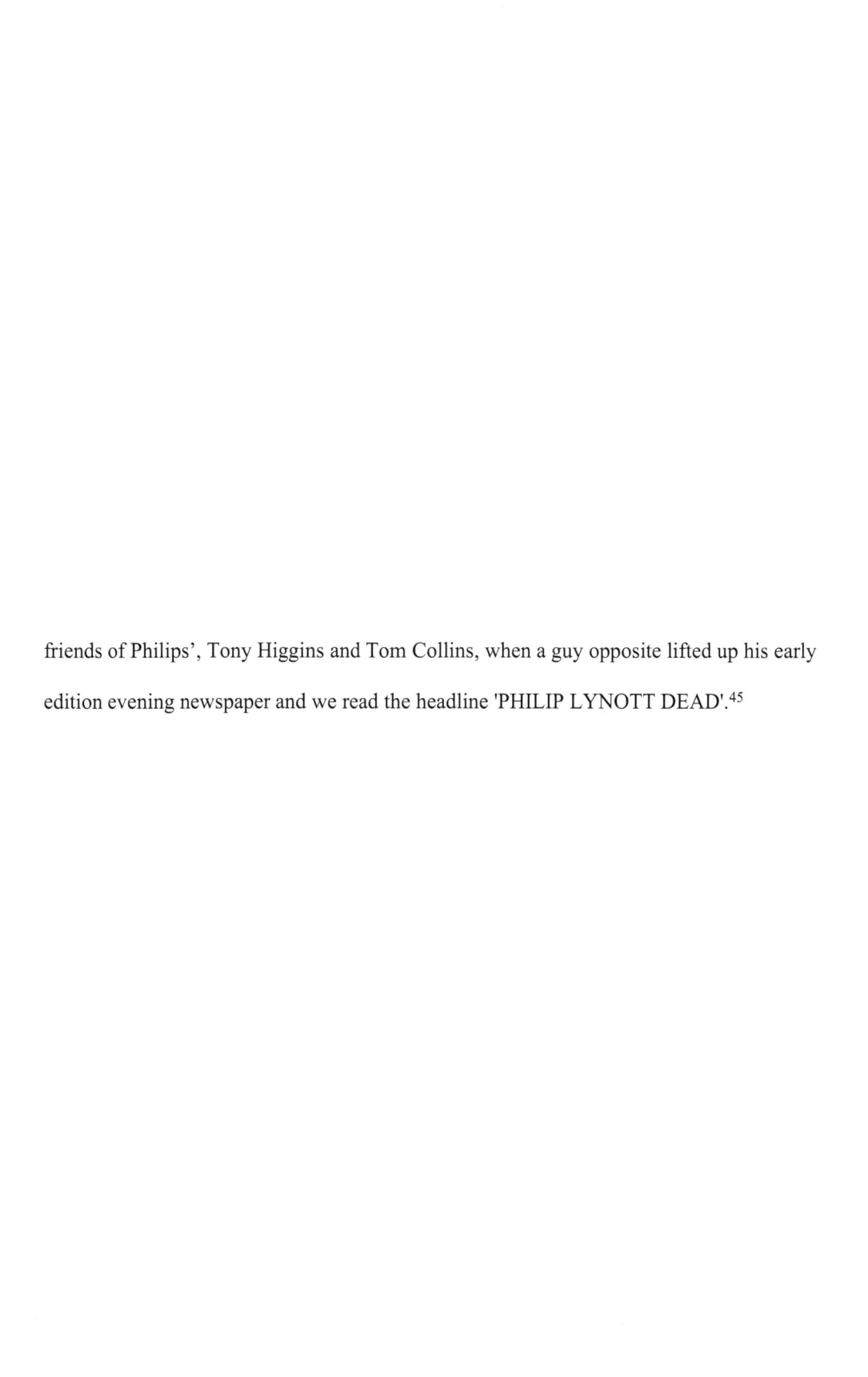

Frank Murray recalled the chilling effects of having to fly his friend's body back to Dublin, "That was one of the saddest moments of my life. Making his last journey, I remember realizing that his coffin was in the hold and I kind of froze in the plane. It was very sad, bringing your buddy home, and normally it would be your guitars and your cases in there. We'd flown around the world together and we'd come back to Ireland lots of times together from tours. Normally there was a sense of joy and celebration and mischief on the plane, we were gonna go to Neary's for a pint. All of a sudden to have the tables turned this way, it was such a sad occasion." Murray last saw Phil in August and remembered him to be in good form, "He seemed to see some light at the end of the tunnel. What he did afterward between then and Christmas, I do not know. It seems like he got an infection and I imagine this would all have been as a result of physical abuse over the years. His immune system was shot to pieces. He couldn't fight what was going on in his body. It's a terribly, terribly sad story for me because it was my friend. The whole nation loved him." Phil's childhood friend and the only drummer Thin Lizzy ever had Brian Downey has stated clearly that Phil's and eventually Lizzy's demise could be summed up with one word – heroin, "Well I think it did destroyed the band. There's no doubt about it. Destroyed the band completely. When heroin gets in, that affects your ability to play rather than anything else. I personally, physically after I tried it couldn't play. I learned that after four or five weeks of being on it that this wasn't for me and I stopped and never taken it since." Scott claims that golf saved his life and helped him fill the massive hole that his heroin addiction had carved out for him. He recalls to the BBC one of the pivotal moments that shook him out of his addicted slumber and how Thin Lizzy meant something more to Phil than just another band:

Crunch time for me came, we were playing some massive festival and I remember not wanting to go on the stage. I was absolutely out of my box. I started to think about that. My whole life you work yourself to get in these positions where you have always wanted to be in, and now you want to do it because you're not stoned enough. And I thought this just ain't right and I remember looking over at Phil and he just had this horribly depressed look on his face and you know he was sweating anyway but it actually looked like tears were coming down because the pain was so bad and I thought oh man this is wrong we gotta fix this…I do know that band was his whole life. He invested a lot of his life into that band. As we all did, but for Phil it was something way deeper. He just loved that band he just loved Thin Lizzy.

Despite snubbing them for Live Aide Bob Geldof said about Thin Lizzy, "It's not just me imagining they were superb, they were." And Midge Ure respectfully makes clear "Lizzy built a bridge from Ireland into the UK and then onto the rest of the world and that bridge has been used by many, many Irish bands. There's no doubt U2 owe them a huge debt of gratitude. They paved the way." From the January 13th, 1986 edition of the Irish Times:

THE CHURCH of the Assumption in Howth, Co Dublin, was packed to overflowing for the funeral Mass for the man described as the father of Irish rock, Phil Lynott, who died in an English hospital a week earlier aged 35. The mourners were led by his wife, Caroline, his two daughters, Sarah and Cathleen, and his mother, Mrs. Phyllis Lynott. There was a large gathering of musicians, business acquaintances, friends and fans, all of who braved a bitter wind to pay tribute to the man who helped put Ireland on the rock-and-roll map…In his homily, the Rev Brian D'Arcy said that Lynott's death would not destroy the memories of him or his music. Father D'Arcy recalled how the Crumlin-born star had paved the way for the success of other Irish acts like U2 and the Boomtown Rats. Bono and Bob Geldof – both of whom were present – would acknowledge the help received from Lynott. The lessons were read by the musician's uncle, Mr. Peter Lynott, and his father-in-law, Mr. Leslie Crowther, the TV presenter. Mr. Crowther's reading from Romans included an obvious reference to some of the more odious publicity over the last week: "You should never pass judgment on a brother or treat him with contempt, as some of you have done." A local traditional group, Clann Eadair, whom Phil Lynott had helped, played throughout the Mass. Their piper, Leo Rickard, played a final lament at the graveside in St Fintan's Cemetery. The large attendance included Phil Lynott's long-time friend and colleague, Brian Downey, and the former Thin Lizzy guitarists, Scott Gorham and John Sykes. Former manager, Mr. Ted Carroll, and former road manager, Mr. Frank Murray, were also there, as were other members of Thin Lizzy's management team in the past, Chris Morrison, Chris O'Donnell and John Salter. The artist, Jim Fitzpatrick, who designed many of the band's record covers, was also among the mourners.[46]

Some revealing moments from one of Phil's last ever interviews given to Hot Press:

Tony Clayton-Lea: Do rock n' roll stars ever grow up?

Philip Lynott: I think people who entertain grow up...You know when you look at yourself in the future? I'd like to think that at a certain age, I'd have written a book, have a nice little place in Howth, on Sundays I'd go down and play in the jazz band, y'know? Have two very exuberant daughters, one an athlete with a gold medal...To become wise about a subject means you must have been a fool at some time. I don't actually think you become wiser, you just get more experienced. And if you have happy times, there have been sad times. There is, however, a price to pay for the good times. I still enjoy playin' a guitar in front of a mirror, posin'.[47]

Sadly because of his losing battle to drug addiction the world was never given a Phil Lynott novel but the music thankfully never died. Thin Lizzy's music is as popular as it ever was and has managed for some unknown magical reason to remain timeless. With original members Scott and Brian overseeing the remastering and mixing process of the Thin Lizzy reissue albums and the announcement that over 700 unheard and over 200 unreleased Thin Lizzy songs had been discovered in a Dublin attic, the Lizzy flag will continue to fly high and inspire generations to come. Thin Lizzy even made front page news in America during the 2012 presidential elections campaign when Republican party nominee entered to the tune of "The Boys are Back in Town". This caused Philomena and Phil's widow Caroline to immediately issue a cease and decease order on the grounds that Phil would NEVER have supported Mitt Romney or share his same political views.

As time marches on so does Phil's legacy. In 2005, a life-size bronze statue of Phil was unveiled on his old stomping grounds near Grafton Street in Dublin. There isn't any statues of rock stars in Ireland so the unveiling ceremony was a grand affair for the city and attended by former band members Gary Moore, Eric Bell, Robbo, Brian Downey, Scott Gorham, Darren Wharton and of course Philomena. The attending Thin Lizzy members paid tribute with a live jam and all of Dublin celebrated their legendary native son. Every year the popular Vibe for Philo commemoration and Poetry exhibitions in Phil's honor remain popularly attended events. His gravesite at St. Fintan's Cemetery in Sutton, northeast Dublin, is a regular Thin Lizzy pilgrimage visited by family, friends, fans and almost daily by Philomena.

Phil's mother still has a hard time accepting that Phil is no longer around and is shocked daily by the throngs of admirers that come from all over the world to pay honor to her only child. And although a tragic figure Phil's legacy remains as an important reminder to not only the power of how poetry and music can have a healthy and everlasting impact on the human soul but also is a sad reminder of the dangers of drug abuse. This book is a testament to Philip Lynott and Thin Lizzy's amazing contribution to the musical and poetical worlds and it's the intention of the author to make sure Thin Lizzy's vast amounts of musical treasures continue to be enjoyed for generations to come. At the same time the book is a warning to other artists to look upon Phil's life as a cautionary tale to the dangers of drug abuse. Hopefully, this book will have some impact on spreading these messages and drive the point across to the executives at the rock n' roll Hall of Fame. Thin Lizzy should take their rightful place on the vaunted establishment's walls and be inducted into the rock n' roll Hall of Fame. This would be a fitting and deserved capping of Thin Lizzy and Phil's legacy. After all it's been more than forty-five years since Thin Lizzy was electrified into creation and there's denying that we're still in love with you.

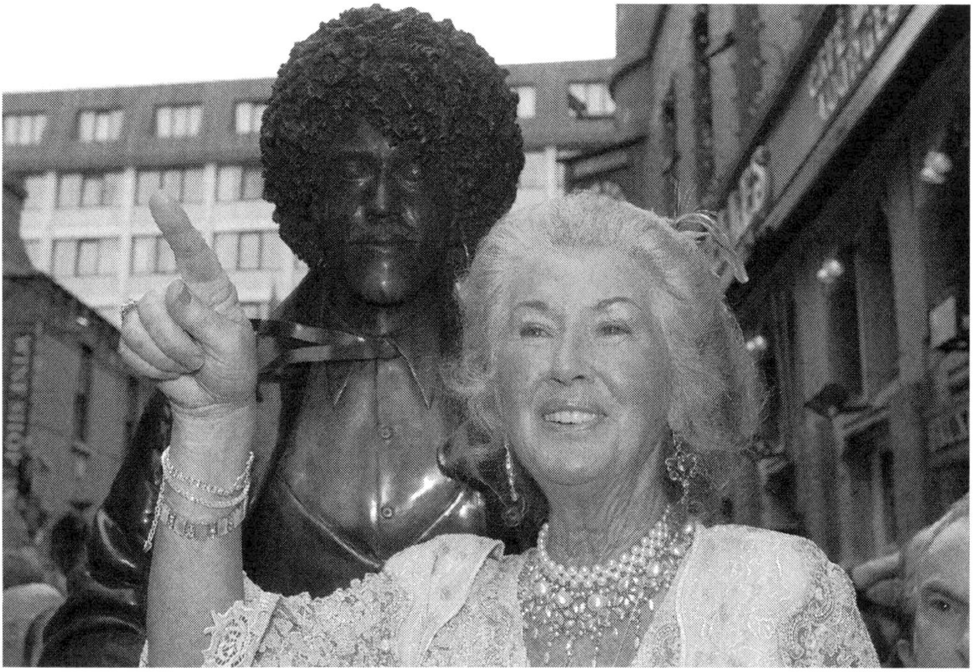

Notes

1. War and Navy departments, Washington D.C., "The Pocket Guide to Northern Ireland" United States Army, 1942, pp.1-2 http://www.belfasthistory.org/pocket-guide-to-northern-ireland-issued-to-american-troops-stationed-in-northern-ireland-during-the-second-world-war/

2. Jason O'Toole, "Philomena Lynott overcame extraordinary odds to raise her beloved 'only boy'. Now she tells of the second son and daughter she gave up for adoption - and why she kept them secret for 50 years" Daily Mail, July 25, 2010 http://www.dailymail.co.uk/femail/article-1297458/Philomena-Lynott-overcame-extraordinary-raise-beloved-boy--Now-tells-second-son-daughter-gave-adoption--kept-secret-50-years.html

3. Guns n' Roses History http://ladydairhean.0catch.com/Axl/history.htm

4. "Thin Lizzy Song F.A.Q. Site – Vagabonds of the Western World" http://www.philip-lynott.com/Vagabond/faqsite/vagabondsofthewesternworld.htm

5. Martin Popoff, "Fighting my way back – Thin Lizzy 69-76" http://www.thinlizzyguide.com/martin_popoff.htm

6. Stephen Thomas Erlewine, "Nightlife" Allmusic.com http://www.allmusic.com/album/night-life-mw0000202880

7. Ann Bixby, "Phil Lynott & Thin Lizzy" http://areuonsomething.com/print_lizzy.html

8. "Thin Lizzy Song F.A.Q. Site – Wild one" http://www.philip-lynott.com/Vagabond/faqsite/fighting.htm

9. Stephen Thomas Erlewine, "Fighting" Allmusic.com
http://www.allmusic.com/album/fighting-mw0000654909

10. "Thin Lizzy Song F.A.Q. Site – The Boys are back in town" http://www.philip-lynott.com/Vagabond/faqsite/jailbreak.htm

11. "Thin Lizzy Song F.A.Q. Site – Cowboy song" http://www.philip-lynott.com/Vagabond/faqsite/jailbreak.htm

12. "Thin Lizzy Song F.A.Q. Site – Emerald" http://www.philip-lynott.com/Vagabond/faqsite/jailbreak.htm

13. Alan Byrne, "Thin Lizzy" Fire Fly Publishing, London, England, 2004, pp.96

14. John Ingham, "Thin Lizzy: Fat Cheque For Thin Men?" Sounds, July 3, 1976 http://jonh-ingham.blogspot.com/2011/03/thin-lizzy-fat-cheque-for-thin-men.html

15. Glenn Rivera, "Giorgio Moroder on the opening day of the film festival Munich" http://glennrivera.multiply.com/journal/item/546/INTERVIEW-Giorgio-Moroder-on-the-opening-day-of-the-film-festival-Munich-

16. "Thin Lizzy Song F.A.Q. Site – Don't believe a word" http://www.philip-lynott.com/Vagabond/faqsite/johnnythefox.htm

17. "Thin Lizzy Song F.A.Q. Site – Massacre" http://www.philip-lynott.com/Vagabond/faqsite/johnnythefox.htm

18. Darryl Smyers, "Huey Lewis: "Phil Lynott Taught Me Most of What I Know"" Dallas Observer, July 20, 2012
http://blogs.dallasobserver.com/dc9/2012/07/huey_lewis_i_am_smart_unbeliev.php

19. "BBC Four – Legends - Thin Lizzy: Bad Reputation" YouTube
    http://www.youtube.com/watch?v=_DXllwgeSCQ

20. Harry Doherty, "The Year Queen Lizzy Shook America" Melody Maker, 1977
    http://www.queenarchives.com/index.php?title=Group_-_XX-XX-1977_-_Melody_Maker

21. Alan Byrne, "Thin Lizzy" Fire Fly Publishing, London, England, 2004, pp.107

22. Kathy Fennessy, "Tony Visconti remembers Thin Lizzy" The Stranger, April 3, 2012
    http://lineout.thestranger.com/lineout/archives/2012/04/03/tony-visconti-remembers-thin-lizzy

23. "The Album 'Bad Reputation' carried a track called 'Soldier of Fortune' Here Phil answers how it came about" Circus, September 29, 1977 http://www.mercenary-wars.net/angola/thin-lizzy.html

24. "Thin Lizzy Song F.A.Q. Site – Soldier of fortune" http://www.philip-lynott.com/Vagabond/faqsite/badreputation.htm

25. "Thin Lizzy Song F.A.Q. Site – Bad reputation" http://www.philip-lynott.com/Vagabond/faqsite/badreputation.htm

26. Ann Bixby, "Phil Lynott & Thin Lizzy" http://areuonsomething.com/print_lizzy.html

27. Stephen Thomas Erlewine, "Bad Reputation" Allmusic.com
    http://www.allmusic.com/album/bad-reputation-mw0000308292

28. Matt Blackett, "Brian Robertson Puts the Live Back in Live and Dangerous" Guitarplayer.com, http://www.guitarplayer.com/article/brian-robertson-puts-the-live-back-in-live-and-dangerous/147543

29. Tony Visconti, "Thin Lizzy: Live & Dangerous" http://www.tonyvisconti.com/artists/thinlizzy/live.htm

30. Nick Kent, "Live and Dangerous" New Musical Express, June 3, 1978 http://www.philip-lynott.com/Vagabond/faqsite/liveanddangerous.htm

31. Neil McCormick, "Phil Lynott almost forgotten rock God" The Telegraph, March 2, 2011 http://www.telegraph.co.uk/culture/music/rockandpopfeatures/8357213/Phil-Lynott-almost-forgotten-rock-god.html

32. "BBC Four – Legends - Thin Lizzy: Bad Reputation" YouTube http://www.youtube.com/watch?v=_DXllwgeSCQ

33. Alan Byrne, "Thin Lizzy" Fire Fly Publishing, London, England, 2004, pp.129

34. Greg Prato, "Black Rose" Allmusic.com http://www.allmusic.com/album/black-rose-a-rock-legend-mw0000199766

35. Alan Byrne, "Thin Lizzy" Fire Fly Publishing, London, England, 2004, pp.106

36. "Phil Lynott talks about his drug problem" YouTube

37. Alan Byrne, "Thin Lizzy" Fire Fly Publishing, London, England, 2004, pp.106

38. Paul du Noyer, "Interview with Phil Lynott" NME, July 5, 1980 http://www.pauldunoyer.com/pages/journalism/journalism_item.asp?journalismID=306

39. "My Irish pub date with Che -- and my tears for Phil Lynott" Independent.ie, September 15, 2012 http://www.independent.ie/lifestyle/my-irish-pub-date-with-che-and-my-tears-for-phil-lynott-3229573.html

40. Thin Lizzy Song F.A.Q. Site – Chinatown" http://www.philip-lynott.com/Vagabond/faqsite/chinatown.htm

41. Ann Bixby, "Phil Lynott & Thin Lizzy" http://areuonsomething.com/print_lizzy.html

42. Paul du Noyer, "Interview with Phil Lynott" NME, July 5, 1980

   http://www.pauldunoyer.com/pages/journalism/journalism_item.asp?journalismID=306

43. Alan Byrne, "Thin Lizzy" Fire Fly Publishing, London, England, 2004, pp.170

44. Ibid

45. "Thin Lizzy Song F.A.Q. Site – Yellow pearl" http://www.philip-lynott.com/Vagabond/faqsite/philiplynottalbum%20.htm

46. Pete Makowski, "Thin Lizzy: back in the Fight" Kerrang! Issue no.34, Jan-Feb, 1983

   http://hearrockcity.blogspot.com/2012/01/klassik-kerrang.html

47. Tony Clayton-Lea, "Philip Lynott interview" Hot Press, May 4, 1984

   http://www.hotpress.com/431546.html

Printed in Poland
by Amazon Fulfillment
Poland Sp. z o.o., Wrocław